A Study of English

Learning and Teaching the Language

A Study of English

Learning and Teaching the Language

DR W. A. GATHERER

Chief Adviser, Lothian

HEINEMANN EDUCATIONAL BOOKS
LONDON

Heinemann Educational Books Ltd
22 Bedford Square, London WC1B 3HH

LONDON EDINBURGH MELBOURNE AUCKLAND
HONG KONG SINGAPORE KUALA LUMPUR NEW DELHI
IBADAN NAIROBI JOHANNESBURG
EXETER(NH) KINGSTON PORT OF SPAIN

British Library C.I.P. Data

Gatherer, William Alexander
A study of English.
1. English language
I. Title
420   PE1072

ISBN 0-435-10369-5

Text set in 10/11 pt Photon Baskerville, printed and bound
in Great Britain at The Pitman Press, Bath

Contents

Preface

You cannot call a book *What teachers, parents and students ought to know about the English language and how it is learned and how it should be taught,* and yet that is what this book is about. Hardly anything in the book is original; yet I do not know of any other book that sets out to bring together the different kinds of information and insights which make up the sum total of what I attempt to say here. That, of course, is why I have written the book.

The English language is many things to many different people. It is a fascinating object of study, whether you look at it historically or as a present-day phenomenon. It is the chief tool we use as native speakers in all our social intercourse. It is an instrument of thought. It is the treasure-house of the world's greatest literature. It is the most widely used language the world has ever known. It is the most important subject in the school curriculum and, for many, the most difficult. To learn English sufficiently to 'get by' is easy for foreigners; to master English is, for many native speakers, often a bitterly forlorn hope.

In describing the nature, origins and history of the language I have tried to put it into an educational perspective, to lay down lines, as it were, that link up our present-day concerns with effective communication and teaching. By giving brief descriptions of modern theoretical and practical researches dealing with language learning I have tried to provide the reader with two aids to better learning and teaching: firstly, the knowledge and understanding we need to underpin our decisions and actions as teaching adults; and secondly, the assurance we gain from being aware that there are insights but no certainties, guidelines but no panaceas. By giving accounts of how English skills are developed, I try to provide the reader with practical help in teaching the young, whether it be teaching children at home or in the classroom. By discussing various aspects of English, such as the notions of correctness and standards that inhabit many of our everyday controversies, I try to share with the reader some of the reassurance that can be derived only from a combination of academic knowledge and practical experience. Having had a long acquaintanceship with the English language as student, parent and educator, I believe that both are necessary – the academic knowledge being a kind of soil in which the practical experience can be nourished. I hope this book will contribute towards the reader's knowledge and experience of language, and at the same time give some hours of pleasure.

W. A. G.

CHAPTER 1

The Nature of Language

Introduction

The study of the nature and history of language finds little place in modern schools, partly for the good reason that teachers are concerned to develop language skills rather than linguistic scholarship. They set out to teach their pupils knowledge *of* English rather than knowledge *about* it. Operational knowledge being so much more important, most teachers wisely decide that there just is not enough time to spare for academic linguistic studies. Another good reason is that children, even in the secondary school, would find the subject very difficult. (It could be taught, though, just as we teach mathematics and history and science, if we thought it worthwhile.) But if the children do not need to be learned in linguistic studies, the adults responsible for their education – teachers and parents – can only benefit from knowing something about what language is and where it comes from.

Communication

It is strange that so much is said about language every day by people who have no very clear idea of what language is. We tell our children to 'Watch your language!' if we hear them speaking in any way we think offensive. We speak of 'the language of the body' when admiring a dancer's movements, and of 'the language of animals' or 'the language of mathematics'. In most of these usages the meaning of *language* is assumed to be 'communication': we think of language as a means of communicating, and anything that *can* be communicated – feelings, moods, ideas, information – can be conveyed by means of language. We also tend to assume that *a language* will be a system of meaningful signs or symbols, so that 'the language' of birds or of ballet or anything else consists of unitary movements or noises or shapes which, when put together, convey a 'message' of some sort.

Students of language have to avoid using the term *language* loosely in that way. We must realize that language is the peculiar, unique phenomenon that we humans – and we alone of all the creatures in the known universe – use to communicate with one another. Any other use of the word is metaphorical: when we speak of 'the language of dance' or 'the language of animals' we mean that these have forms of communication that *resemble* – that possess some of the characteristics of – human language. Of course the communication systems of some animal species are complex and subtly patterned, and the study of non-linguistic communication (*semiotics*) has shown that some quite powerful signalling systems exist in nature. Scientists can create signalling systems which perform many of the functions of language. The recent work of American psychologists with chimpanzees, for example, shows that many gestural conventions can be devised to convey meaning between man and animal; for centuries shepherds have contrived fairly elaborate signalling systems for their dogs. A recently invented sign system called *Amerind* (because it is derived from American Indian signs) makes it possible for speechless persons, such as throat cancer patients, to convey quite complex concepts and messages by means of 250 hand-signs and agglutinations, or chains, of the signs.

What makes human language different from most other communication systems is that language employs *symbols*, not *signs*. A sign is a token, a mark or device that carries a special meaning, or has a specific meaning attached to it. Animal noises, such as purring, snarling or barking, are signs of the animal's feelings. A physical movement can be a sign: a nod, a wink, a pout, a smile. Some signs can be used to convey a meaning, for example miming the lifting of a spoon to the mouth, or rubbing one's stomach. But human language uses *arbitrary symbols:* signs, if you like, which represent things only because they have been selected to do so. Symbols are *conventional signs,* like the shapes on maps which signify railways, churches or golf-courses. Language consists of arbitrary symbols. In so far as the signs learned by Washoe, the chimpanzee trained by Professor and Mrs Gardner,* were capable of being combined to form sentences, they constituted language.

Many people find it hard to accept that the symbols of language are arbitrary – that is, that they have no intrinsic, natural or inevitable meaning embodied in them. The symbols of language, the sounds and words we use when we speak, are wholly conventional signs: they mean what they do mean only because people agree that that is what they mean. You may remember the old joke about the Italian who invented spaghetti. When asked why he called it *spaghetti*,

* R. A. and B. T. Gardner described their work in 'Teaching sign language to a chimpanzee' in *Science*, 165, pp. 664–72.

he said, 'Because it looks like spaghetti, it feels like spaghetti, and it tastes like spaghetti'. And there is the character in Aldous Huxley's *Crome Yellow* who, looking at some pigs, says 'Rightly is they called *pigs*'. These are examples of a common tendency to confuse the linguistic symbol with the thing it symbolizes. In fact, the arbitrary nature of linguistic symbols can easily be seen when we look at the words used in different languages to mean the same thing: a horse is a horse all over the world, but the English word *horse* is just as arbitrary a symbol for that animal as the French *cheval*, the Greek *hippos*, the Latin *equus*, the German *Pferd* or the Russian *kon'*.

Many languages do have examples, however, of attempts to represent an actual sound by means of language. This is *onomatopoeia*, a device that people have always enjoyed using. Onomatopoetic words like *swoosh, click, dingdong* do to some extent imitate reality. But even with this phenomenon the arbitrariness of linguistic symbology can be shown by comparing the different word-sounds used for the same noises in different languages: for example a German cock crows *Kikeriki*, not *cock-a-doodle-do*, and a French cat goes *ron-ron*, not *purr-purr*; in German a door banging is represented by *Knapps* and a bell ringing by *Bim-Bam*. Also, it can be shown that identical *sounds* may have completely different meanings in different languages: for example, *Rock* means 'jacket' in German, and in Russian *rok* means 'fate', and in Czech the same sound means 'year'. Again, the effect of Tennyson's line 'the murmuring of innumerable bees' is entirely dependent on the meaning, even though we may feel that it does represent the drowsy sounds of a summer afternoon. If we make a slight phonetic change to 'the murdering of innumerable beeves' we completely destroy the imitative effect.[1] Nevertheless sound-imitation exists in most languages, and yields such words as *cuckoo, tinkle, pingpong* which undeniably reflect actuality. Sound-painting is also evident in poetry from ancient Greek to modern English and this is the deliberate creation of a sound pattern which in some way brings actual noises to mind: for example, Wilfred Owen's lines:

> Only the stuttering rifles' rapid rattle
> Can patter out their hasty orisons.

And then there is a phenomenon called *sound symbolism* or sound metaphor. In many languages, certain sounds have come to express certain qualities: for example in French clear vowels can express smallness, and in English the syllable *unk* can express something contemptible, as in *junk, bunkum, clunk* and so on.

Despite all these examples – which are merely exceptions to prove the rule – language normally employs arbitrary symbols. These symbols are primarily sounds – the units of speech.

The Sound System

It has been suggested that language can be thought of as *organized noise*,[2] and most linguists agree that speech is the primary substance of language. Speech comes first, in the history of mankind and in the growth of language in the individual. Speech is by far the most frequently and most widely used form of language; all the writing that ever existed is but a thin spume on a sea of speech. Indeed, many linguists have asserted that language *is* speech, that written language is merely speech recorded on paper. Writing, however, as we shall see, is a distinctly different mode of using language, with its own rules and characteristic features. If it is speech-written-down, it is speech transmuted into something other than speech.

Language, then, is organized noise: noise produced by a vocal apparatus that only human beings possess. The sound substance, or phonology, of a language consists of a finite number of identifiable units called *phonemes*. A phoneme is a minimal *significant* sound: that is to say, the phoneme makes the difference between the meaning of a word as against any other word. For example, it is the initial phoneme which contrasts the meaning of *bin* and *pin, tin* and *chin*. The linguist recognizes the sounds /b/, /p/, /t/, and /ch/ as distinctive features: each is a phoneme. The middle and end sounds, /i/ and /n/, are also phonemes. So the word *pin* consists of three phonemes. A phoneme, however, must not be equated with a letter: a phoneme is a phonological unit, while a letter is an alphabetic unit. Note that the same letter can have different sounds when occurring at different places. In the word *pip*, the initial [p] is a different sound from the final [p]; in the word *spin* the [p] is different again in sound. These are *phonetic* differences, but they are all instances (or allophones) of the phoneme /p/, because they provide the same kind of contrast with other phonemes.*

All languages employ a range of between 15 and 50 phonemes. English uses about 46 phonemes; the precise number cannot be stated because some dialects of English use phonemes which do not occur in others. Russian uses about 43 phonemes, French and German about 35. The identification of the phonemes employed by different languages is not a useful exercise, since the term *phoneme* is used to classify sounds that perform similar functions within one language. *Phoneme*, indeed, is a term which most linguists use as a convenience without necessarily agreeing as to its precise meaning.

Phonemes are classified into consonants and vowels, and they go

---

*Linguists write allophones between square brackets [ ] and phonemes between oblique brackets / /.

together to form syllables. A syllable is a phonological unit; that is, it is part of the phonology, or sound system, of language. The phonological system also has features of stress and intonation which linguists are busy analysing and describing.

The Grammatical System

There is another system in language – the system of grammar. This has to do with the way we order the symbols of language to create meaning. The smallest units of grammar are not phonemes, for these inhabit only the sound system and have no distinctive meaning in the normal sense of that term.

Most people unacquainted with linguistics would think of a word as the smallest unit of the grammatical system. But many words are divisible into smaller meaningful units. The linguist calls this smallest unit a *morpheme*. Like the phoneme, the morpheme is not a universally agreed concept, but it is a useful notion in linguistic analysis. The morpheme is the smallest individually meaningful unit in an utterance. The word *uneatable*, for example, can be divided into three morphemes, *un*, *eat* and *able*. Every word consists of one or more morphemes. A *free morpheme* is one that can constitute a word by itself; a *bound morpheme* (for example, *un-*, *dis-*, *-ise*) never occurs alone, being always bound to at least one other morpheme. In the word *uneatable, -able* is a bound morpheme, though it may appear to be a free morpheme; but it is not the same morpheme as the free form *able* in such an utterance as *he is able*. Morphemes can also be classified as *roots* and *affixes* (prefixes and suffixes), an affix being a bound morpheme used to extend or modify the meaning of a word, and a root being either a bound or a free morpheme which remains when the affixes have been removed from a given word. For example, in *uneatable, un-* and *-able* are affixes, and *eat* is the root. In the word *intolerable, in-* and *-able* are obviously bound morphemes, but what is left, *-toler-* is obviously not a free morpheme, so this word consists of three bound morphemes, *-toler-* being the root. Every word 'contains' a root, though many words consist entirely of a single root.

But what exactly is a word? This is one of the most difficult questions in the study of language. Aristotle defined a word as 'the smallest significant unit of speech', but as we have seen that role is now reserved for the morpheme. The meaning of the word *significant*, too, is a difficulty, since it is extremely hard to define *meaning*. Definitions relying on meaning are not acceptable to many linguists. Leonard Bloomfield, the American pioneer of modern linguistics, gives the classic definition of a word as a *minimum free form*, that is a unit which can have meaning when used alone. But as Otto Jespersen, the great Danish grammarian, pointed out, there are many forms which are not free which are given the status of word. For example, French *je* and Russian *K* ('towards') are not free forms; and in English *a* and *the* do not normally occur as free forms. Bloomfield also proposes that a word can be characterized as a form which cannot be 'interrupted' by another form. For example, a phrase such as *sit there* can be interrupted by inserting a preposition – *sit over there* – or an adverb – *sit quietly there*. But neither *sit* nor *there* can have another form intelligibly inserted in it. You cannot say *si-over-t* or *the-over-re*. This would appear to be an unquestionable characterization of a word. But even this 'rule' can be broken in English, for like Eliza Doolittle in *My Fair Lady* you can say *abso-blooming-lutely*.*

The academic difficulty about defining a word comes from the differences in the different systems of language. It is easy enough to define a word in terms of written English: it is what normally occurs between the spaces in print. But what lies behind the accepted conventions of spacing? It is also easy – at first glance – to accept the 'commonsense' conception of a word as the smallest speech unit capable of functioning as a complete utterance. But what is a complete utterance? If you ask someone to speak very slowly, you will hear them separating off forms which we would not accept as words: for example, *Allofa . . . sudden . . . theman . . . gavea . . . scream*. In normal talk we seldom separate 'words': we join them together to form longer units such as breath-groups. And to define a word in terms of meaning is just as unsatisfactory: as Jespersen pointed out, what makes *triangle* a word and *three-sided figure formed by lines* not a word?

'The only unimpeachable definition of a word', said Jespersen, 'is that it is a human habit, an habitual act on the part of one human individual which has, or may have, the effect of evoking some idea in the mind of another individual'.³ Fortunately, it is a habit all human beings seem to share: the recognition of the word as a unit is a universally held ability. We have an intuitive awareness of 'wordness'.

It is, however, the absence of objective definition for words that makes the notions of the phoneme and morpheme so useful. It is best to think of the phoneme as a unit in the system of phonology in language, and the morpheme as a unit in the system of grammar. The word can then be described as a combination, in the phonology, of phonemes and, in the grammar, of morphemes. The relationships of

* 'Oh wouldn't it be lovely
  Oh so lovely sitting abso-blooming-lutely still.'

morphemes within the structure of words is the study of morphology. The combining of words into larger structures is syntax. Grammar can thus be divided into morphology and syntax. Its units are morphemes, words, phrases and sentences. Morphemes come together to make words, words combine to form phrases, and phrases combine to form sentences. This is a taxonomy, a scheme of arrangements in which each unit is contained in the next larger class of units.

Syntax is the arrangement of words to make up phrases and sentences. The description of syntax requires the classification of words according to their function, and an account of their relations to one another. Words are grammatically classified in various ways, according to the grammatical theory held. Traditionally words were said to fall into eight 'parts of speech' – nouns, verbs, adjectives, adverbs, pronouns, prepositions, conjunctions and articles. Jespersen listed six parts of speech; other linguists have identified ten and yet others as many as nineteen. Different accounts of grammar have different categories because the grammarians use different methods of analysis.

One of the most useful distinctions among words is that between 'class' words and 'function' words. 'Class' words form an *open set*, that is, there can be no end to the number of words which can be substituted for them in a grammatically acceptable utterance. For example, in the sentence frame

///The//   //is//   ///*

the blank spaces can be filled by an infinite number of possibilities. (Even if it were possible to list all the known words ever invented one could go on and on inventing words which would be grammatically acceptable.) On the other hand, 'function' words form a *closed system*; that is, there is a definite number of words classifiable under each label. For example, in the sentence frame

/// The / little / boy // in / the / park // kicked / the / ball ///

only prepositions can logically replace *in*,[4] and there is a finite number of these in any language; and only a few words (determiners such as *a, this, that*) could intelligibly be substituted for *the*.

Syntactic structure can be described in various ways, and different grammatical theories demonstrate different techniques. In the traditional grammar developed during the eighteenth and nineteenth centuries a sentence was said to consist of three main elements, the subject, the predicator and the object, and these were identified as

* The oblique strokes are conventions used by linguists to mark off units in the sentence.

single key words. For example, in the sentence *The two black cats chased the poor little mouse* the subject is *cats*, the predicator is *chased* and the object is *mouse*. A different grammar, however, would say that the subject is *The two black cats*, and that the object is *the poor little mouse*. According to this grammar, each is a *noun phrase*, and can be further analyzed into the *head word* (*cats, mouse*) and *modifiers* (*the, two, black, the, poor, little*). A third grammatical approach is to divide each construction into binary pattern parts or *immediate constituents*. Thus the sentence would be said to consist of two parts: *The two black cats* and *chased the poor little mouse*. The predicate would be cut into two immediate constituents (called ICs): *chased* and *the poor little mouse*. The ICs of the noun phrase in the predicate are *the* and *poor little mouse;* then we have *poor* and *little mouse* and finally *little* and *mouse*.

These are merely a few examples of a complex and difficult pursuit, namely the grammatical analysis of a sentence. Literally thousands of attempts have been made to produce new and better grammars of given languages, and linguists all over the world are preoccupied by this enthralling subject. Since we all possess and operate grammatical theories of one sort or another it is important to understand what grammar is and does, and in Chapter 4 I shall take up the subject of grammar from the educational point of view.

The Semantic System[5]

We have seen that language can be analyzed to reveal a phonological system and a grammatical system. A third system which has been postulated by linguists is the semantic system, by which the meanings of words and sentences are realized. Theories of meaning have aroused controversy for centuries and although there have been genuine advances made since the mid-sixties we still lack a coherent and well-established semantic theory. This is not surprising since the subject involves linguistics, anthropology, psychology and even philosophy in its content and techniques.

A semantic description of language concentrates on the meaning of lexical items. The difference between a grammatical component and a lexical component of a sentence can be seen if we consider the sentence *My uncle has to put up with a lot of nagging.* As we have seen, some of these words are members of a closed system (*has, to, up, with, a, of*) so that the meaning they carry can be thought of as *grammatical* meaning: they function grammatically in the sentence. The word *to* in the phrase *has to* can be said to have no meaning at all, merely a function. The words *my* and *up* carry greater meaning (that is, *semanticity*) than the words *with* and *a*. The words which carry the greatest semantic loads are those called 'class' words. These are the nouns, verbs, adjectives and adverbs which occur in open sets and which exhibit relationships with one another which have nothing to do with grammar. Semantics is the study of these non-grammatical inter-relationships.

It is more accurate, however, to speak of *lexical items* rather than words. This can be illustrated from our sentence: *put up with* is a phrase, not a word, but it carries a single meaning (similar to the meaning of the word *tolerate*) and can be regarded as a single semantic entity; the same can be said of the phrase *a lot of*, which can be replaced by *much* without any important modification of the meaning of the sentence.

The sum total of the lexical items of a language is called the *dictionary* of the language. I prefer the term *lexicon* because it saves confusion between the linguistic term *dictionary* and the name of the reference list commonly called a dictionary. The lexicon is the mental list of items we all possess corporately as speakers of a language. (Nobody knows the whole lexicon, of course. The words an individual knows are called his vocabulary.) A dictionary, on the other hand, is merely a list of lexical items, mostly words but including phrases and idioms, for each of which the lexicographer proffers some information. This information varies according to the lexicographer's editorial policy, the target readership and so on. It usually comprises lexical information (related to the meaning), grammatical information (related to the part of speech) and etymological information (related to the origin and history of the word). The lexical information given by a dictionary is usually considered to be the 'meaning' of the item. But in fact the term *meaning* is full of ambiguity. A dictionary will give you a number of synonyms, or a scientific definiton, or merely a reference to a more inclusive class for the item. (For example, *dog* can be expressed as 'a four-legged, flesh-eating mammal' or 'a carnivorous quadruped etc.' or 'an animal of the species *dog*'.) None of these can truly be called a lexical definition.

The lexical definition of a word, phrase or idiom is a set of semantic features which *define* the item in the sense of showing its relationships to all other items in the language as well as to the objects and actions in the real world. Of course there is no possibility of creating a dictionary which could give lexical definitions. Semantics has not advanced to that level of proficiency; in any case it would be impossibly large and consequently it would be useless. Semantics scholars are not in the business of lexicography. Their task is to tease out the nature of the meaning of words. A brief account of some of their ideas and techniques will illustrate what semanticists try to do.

In the first place the semanticist is concerned with what in Logic is known as 'analytic' truth, not 'synthetic' truth. Synthetic truth is what is true as a matter of fact, by reference to the world outside language. Analytic truth is what is true by virtue of meaning alone. Thus the sentence *A boy is male* is true because 'being male' is a consequence of the meaning of the word *boy* – there is no need to prove that all boys are male by recourse to reality. Secondly, the semanticist uses 'rules' which attempt to show how the 'semantic competence' of a native speaker of a language can manifest itself in language: that is, in the sounds of language organized by the phonological and grammatical systems. The process of making an utterance (or encoding) can be illustrated thus:

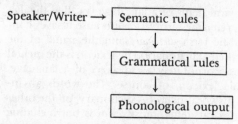

The process of understanding an utterance (or decoding) is roughly the reverse:

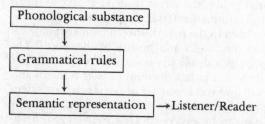

The semantic rules are not psychologically real. They are abstractions invented by the linguist to enable him to analyze the meaning system. But they do represent the operating principles we employ to organize the elements of language into meaningful patterns.

One kind of semantic rule is *meaning postulates*. Examples are:

$$boy \longrightarrow male$$
$$girl \longrightarrow female$$

The arrows represent *implication*: they mean *if ... then*, so that *boy* → *male* means 'if x is a boy, then x is male'. The meaning of a lexical item is specified by the set of all the meaning postulates in which it occurs.

It would be theoretically feasible to provide, by this method, true definitions of words in terms of their semantic features. Other semantic relations can be described by means of showing *negative implication*. For example, *hyponymy*, or 'inclusion', can be shown by the following rules:

(a) x is a tulip ⟶ x is not a rose
     x is a rose ⟶ x is not a tulip
(b) x is a tulip ⟶ x is a flower
     x is a rose ⟶ x is a flower
(c) x is a flower ⟶ either x is a tulip or x is a rose

'Tulip' and 'rose' are said to be co-hyponyms, and 'flower' is the superordinate term of the set. *Antonymy*, or 'oppositeness', and *converseness* are other semantic relationships which can be explicated by means of meaning postulates.

Componential analysis provides semantic rules of another kind. This approach describes distinctive features, called *semantic components*, which are perceived in the vocabulary structure of a language. Semantic components are theoretical elements, not real words. (For this reason they are printed in capital letters.) For example the lexical item *boy* can be said to consist of the components ANIMATE and HUMAN and MALE and not ADULT. Implicational rules can be stated thus:

(a) HUMAN   animate
(b) MALE   not FEMALE
(c) FEMALE   not MALE
(d) MALE   ANIMATE
(e) FEMALE   ANIMATE

And the item *boy* can be specified thus:

boy: ANIMATE and HUMAN and MALE and not FEMALE and not ADULT.

Sets of lexical items whose meanings are related are said to form a 'semantic field'. Kinship terms constitute the semantic field most used by linguists for examples because anthropological studies of kinship yielded the earliest and most elaborate analyses of semantics. Other semantic fields are inhabited by verbs of motion, social roles and so on. Linguists cannot hope to deal with more than a few small subfields since they are still grappling with the formidable task of developing the basic concepts and techniques necessary for analysis. But semanticists are beginning to do for the meaning system of language what grammarians and phonologists have done for the other systems – they are providing precise descriptions and theoretical insights of increasing explanatory power, and in this way they are making a valuable contribution to our understanding of how language works.

The Languages of the World

So far I have referred to 'language' as if it were a universally similar phenomenon, as if all languages were alike. This is obviously not the case. One of the most important facts about language is that its manifestations differ in many ways, with different sound-systems, meaning systems and grammars. There are about 3000 known languages in the world today, with distinct vocabularies, grammatical conventions and pronunciation habits. It would seem that every possible phoneme the human larynx can utter is in use somewhere in some language. Names of common objects vary from language to language in sound and shape. Languages vary enormously, for example, in the way they organize their structures for making statements and asking questions, in the way they indicate tense, mood and number, and in the way they deal with gender.

It has always been the case that people tend to think of their mother tongue as the only one that matters. In many languages the name for foreigners originally meant 'The Stutterers' or 'The Mutes' while the name for the home tribe meant 'The Speakers'. The Greek word 'barbarian' derives from *barbaros*, the stammering babble of foreign speech. The word *Deutsch* originally meant 'The People', as did many other nationality labels. English, we must remind ourselves, comes from the name of the tribe called Angles. We carry this linguistic chauvinism into our daily lives: hence the tendency to find foreigners' speech funny (especially when they try to speak our own tongue), to be surprised when we discover that other languages lack features (such as the definite article, or prepositions) which we take for granted in our own, and to deplore the difficultness of a foreign language's grammar.

The uniqueness of any one language can, however, be exaggerated. For most general characteristics of phonology, grammar and semantics, languages tend to cluster in families. This is not surprising since they developed from common ancestors.

The modern European languages all stem from a language or group of dialects, spoken about 7000 years ago, which we now call Indo-European. So also do most of the languages spoken in the sub-continent of India. This fact was discovered early in the nineteenth century when studies of Sanskrit revealed similarities of structure and vocabulary between this ancient Indian language and the Germanic, Romance and Celtic languages of Europe. Languages which seemed to be vastly different, such as Greek and Latin, English and Russian, German and Welsh, were all found to share a common ancestry. This astonishing discovery came at a time when most people accepted the

Biblical explanation of the origin of language – that all men spoke Hebrew until the Tower of Babel, 'when the Lord did confound the language of all the earth'.*

European languages fall into 'sub-families'. English is one of a *Germanic* group, its fellow members being German, Dutch, Danish, Norwegian, Swedish, Yiddish, Frisian and Icelandic. Another sub-family is the *Romance* group comprising Rumanian, French, Italian, Spanish and Portuguese. Related to this is the *Celtic* group, consisting of Welsh, Breton, Erse and Gaelic. The *Slavic* group comprises Russian, Bulgarian, Polish, Czech, Serbo-Croatian. Modern Greek occupies its own place in the *Indo-European* super-family. Some of the languages of India – Hindi, Urdu, Punjabi, Bengali, Gujerati, Sindhi, Marathi – are Indo-European in origin; but others, such as Tamil, Telegu and other Dravidian languages are members of a different super-family (descended from some common ancestor other than Indo-European). Yet another super-family (the *Sinitic*) comprises the Chinese tongues and others such as Vietnamese, Laotian and Cambodian. Another super-family is the *Semitic* group of which Hebrew and Arabic are the best known. There are hundreds of other language families throughout the world – every continent can be sub-divided many times to show a linguistic geography as varied as its physical geography.

The modern world, however, is dominated by a few languages which are spoken by very large numbers of people: 350 million people speak Chinese, 300 million English, 160 million Hindi, 140 million Russian, 110 million Spanish. Though second to Chinese in the number of speakers, undoubtedly the most widely spoken language in the world is English. Not only is it the first language of the United States, Canada, Australia, New Zealand, Ireland, Rhodesia and the United Kingdom, but it is a dominant language in South Africa, Nigeria, Kenya, India and many other countries. It is the preferred second language learned in the vast majority of countries, only in one or two European countries being secondary to French or German. It has been estimated that 600 million people can use English competently.

Linguistic Universals

Besides the historical similarities that can be perceived in various language groups, there are certain invariant or universal properties

---

* It is said that James IV of Scotland proved that Hebrew was the original tongue by isolating two boys from all human company. They naturally developed Hebrew, according to the report.

which are known to be common to all languages, at any rate to all the languages which have so far been studied by linguists.

One of these is called 'double articulation' or structural duality. This is the presence in every language of two levels of structure: substance and form. The substance of language is the elements, sounds and letters, which make up speech and writing. These elements have no meaning in themselves; meaning inheres only in the 'primary level', which consists of words, phrases and sentences.

Another universal characteristic of language is that all humans seem to possess the ability to invent new utterances in their own language. This 'creativity' was pointed out by Noam Chomsky, the eminent American philosopher-linguist. Chomsky says that every native speaker of a language is able to create an indefinitely large number of sentences, including sentences that cannot ever have been heard before, and this is done without conscious effort. Accounting for this linguistic productivity has become a prime preoccupation of modern linguistics.

Yet another universal property is the conceptual framework which underlies all language. A universal set of semantic categories, such as ANIMATE/INANIMATE, HUMAN/NON-HUMAN and CONCRETE/ABSTRACT can be perceived in all languages. It is this, above all else, that makes it possible to translate one language into another.

Within phonology, certain habits of patterning would seem to be universal. It has been suggested that the same basic set of phonemic elements can be seen to combine in all languages, and that only about a dozen contrastive features operate in any language's phonetic structure. In grammar, certain relations and categories, such as subject and object, nouns, verbs, adjectives and so on, are observable in every language.

Finally, it is a universal characteristic of language that it functions as personal, social and transactional behaviour. All human beings use language for basically the same reasons and purposes. We all express in language our emotions – fears, joys, frustrations, sorrows. We all use it to get on with other human beings – to identify with people, to assert our wills, to link our beings. And we all use language to conduct our everyday business, to record our needs, to fulfil our desires. Whatever the differences in the tongues of men, language makes *homo loquens*, the speaking creature, into *homo sapiens*.

Origins

A passage from *The Quiver*, 1891, entitled 'The Gift of Language', gives what is probably the oldest explanation of how language originated:

> It should never be forgotten that there is no reason whatsoever for regarding language as a human invention, or for supposing that men, if left to themselves, could arrange or employ a system of sounds for communicating their thoughts the one to the other. It is easily inferred from the Scriptural narrative that God gave Adam his vocabulary, as well as that fine intellectual apparatus which might excogitate things worthy of being embodied in its magnificent expressions.

The biblical notion of language as a divine gift is echoed in Egyptian, Babylonian, Chinese and Indian mythology. Most primitive societies would seem to have reached the conclusion that language was peculiar to man, that it was given to him by the divinity, and that consequently it possessed great powers for good and evil. Taboos, spells and other superstitions appear always to have been associated in men's minds with the magicality of words; hence the prevalence of incantations, magic formulae, secret names and so on in folk-lore and legends throughout the centuries.

But for many centuries also men have looked for more rational foundations for language. Plato's dialogue, *Cratylus*, treated such questions as whether names are significant by 'nature' or 'convention', and how far language is an instrument of thought. Aristotle, in the *Poetics*, and in the *Art of Rhetoric*, introduced what has been called 'the foundation of what should have been the brightest instead of the dullest of the sciences' – linguistics.[6] Speculation about the origins of language have appeared in every century, but it was not until the nineteenth century that serious hypotheses appeared in the form of the theories nicknamed by Max Muller. The *bow-wow* theory suggested that language originated in man's imitation of animal noises. The *ding-dong* theory suggested that language came from the imitation of other sounds, such as bells, implying a natural connection between the word sound and the thing referred to – a notion discussed by Plato. The *pooh-pooh* theory proposed that the earliest language came from man's instinctive cries of pain, joy, anger and so on. The *yo-he-ho* theory suggested that it originated in chants as men performed tasks in concert such as dragging logs. Modern linguists tend to discount speculation of this kind on the grounds that there can never be evidence, but it remains a fascinating subject.

Attempts to infer the origin of languages from the tongues of primitive peoples have failed because there seem to be no primitive languages. People tend to think that the simple savage must speak a simple tongue, hence the Red Indian in the Western saying things like

'White man no come' and Tarzan saying 'You Jane, me Tarzan'. But this is not so. However primitive may be the economic or cultural systems of aboriginals, their languages are fully developed and, if anything, more complex than those of western civilization. The great languages like English have become *simpler* over the centuries in grammar and other systemic features.

We know nothing of how man came to develop language, but we know that it happened a long, long time before the Indo-European speakers were born. A very long time – thousands of years – passed before the language we know as Old English came to predominate in Britain. It came into the islands with Low German speakers from the fourth to the sixth centuries AD. The Saxons, Frisians, Angles and Jutes who made up the parent stocks spoke different dialects, and it was not until about the sixth century that the parent tongue of Modern English came to dominate England. It is interesting that although the Angles were a a smaller tribe than the others it was their name, *Angle-ish*, which attached itself to the language; King Alfred, ruler of the West Saxons, wrote of his country as England and of his mother tongue as English. From the fifth to the thirteenth century there were three predominant dialects of English: Northumbrian, Mercian (the progenitor of Modern English) and the Anglo-Saxon of Wessex. After 624 the Celto-Latin alphabet brought by Irish missionaries gave the language a new vitality, or so it would seem from the remarkable literature that has survived. The famous epic poem *Beowulf,* written about 700, and the work of Caedmon, Bede and Alcuin, exhibits a language of great beauty and power.

As might be expected since every living language is always in a state of change, the Old English (or 'Anglo-Saxon') of the period 450 to 1150 was an ever-changing language. The morphology and syntax remained much the same as those of the ancestral Low German dialects, but the lexicon acquired borrowings from the tongues spoken by the Celts of Wales and Ireland, from the Danish and Norse, and from the ecclesiastical Latin of the missionaries and church dignitaries. It was a very different language from Modern English. Here is an example:

Old English

Nu is Crist geboren on ᵹisse• sylfan nihte,
gesaelig Godes bearn, on ᵹaere Davidis byrig,
so goda dryhten.

•ᵹ is a letter which represents the *th* sound.

Modern English

Now is Christ born in this self-same night,
blessed bairn of God, in (the) David's burgh,
the good Lord.

The principal difference, apart of course from lexical items which have long disappeared, is that Modern English is much less inflected. For example Old English used suffixes to indicate the case and gender of nouns: thus *ox* had the forms *oxa* (when used as the subject), *oxan* (when used as the object) and *oxena* (when meaning *of the oxen*). In Modern English these inflections have almost disappeared except in some unusual forms such as *ox, oxen; child, children;* and *brother, brethren.* Old English adjectives were also inflected, whereas in Modern English most adjectives have only one form. Exceptions which preserve the Old English inflections are *olden* and *golden.* In Old English infinitive verbs ended in *-an*, while in Modern English the function word *to* is used as a free form. The Old English orthography (the spelling system) was, as might be expected considering the time which has lapsed, very different even for words which have remained identical, such as *hwaet (what), heofon (heaven), leoht (light).* What has happened to most of the Old English words which have survived into Modern English, however, is simply that their endings have disappeared. During the Middle English period (from about 1150 to about 1500) the endings were all reduced to *-e*, and since then they have been lost altogether. Thus:

Old English	became	Middle English	became	Modern English
mona		moné*		moon
nama		namé		name
withutan		withuté		without
sunu		suné		son
sunne		sunne		sun

The profound changes which occurred in English after the Norman conquest can be characterized as a great simplification of the grammar and an enormous enrichment of the lexicon. By the fourteenth century, when English at last replaced French as the officially recognized language, it had been transformed. The Old English noun inflections had gone, except for the possessive *s*; the adjectives had become simple stems; verbs had become the uninflected forms of Modern English. Because of the long co-existence of French and

* The accent ' above a letter means that it is pronounced.

English, the lexicon had acquired many doublets such as *pork* and *pig*, *mutton* and *sheep*, *calf* and *veal*; *liberty* and *freedom*; *sage* and *wise*; many French words were borrowed to connote military terms, such as *army*, *assault, lieutenant, soldier*; and the French brought in a whole new legal vocabulary, such as *jury, judge, attorney, plaintiff, verdict*, and many others.

By the end of the fourteenth century English had become relatively stable as a language. If one puts Chaucer's English into modern spelling, the language of the *Canterbury Tales*, written about 1388, is not very different from our own:

> Befell that in that season on a day,
> In Southwark at the Tabard as I lay
> Ready to wend on my pilgrimage
> To Canterbury with full devout courage,
> At night was come into that hostelry
> Well nine and twenty in a company ...

Of course there have been many changes in grammar and lexis: habits of speech change with habits of thought and everyday life. But such changes as have occurred since the fourteenth century are trivial compared with the changes that occurred during the four preceding centuries. It was then that the basic framework of the language was built and the changes which have occurred since have been mainly of style and semantic preference.

One important change did, however, occur in the phonology of English from about 1400 onwards. Known as the 'Great English Vowel Shift', this accounts for many of the apparent differences between Modern English and earlier forms of the language. What happened was that changes took place in the way various vowels were normally pronounced. Old English words for *no, cold, old* were pronounced as if to rhyme with *saw*. The Old English words for *deed, seed* would have rhymed with the modern words *paid, laid* as pronounced by a Scot or a Welshman. Similar changes occurred with other vowels. These changes are regular: certain Old English vowels have been replaced in every instance with the same sound in Modern English. Another change was the diphthongization of vowels. A diphthong is two vowels merged, pronounced in one syllable. Thus Old English vowels, such as in *hus* (rhyming with *loose*) or *wif* (rhyming with *reef*) have come to sound like *house* or *wife*.

These changes have made the sound system of English different from that of any other European language. But some speakers of English, such as the Scots and Welsh, have preserved many of the old 'pure' vowels, so that their oral reading of Shakespeare, for example, would sound more like his own pronunciation. For similar historical reasons the original *ch* sound in words like *night, light* has given way to a diphthong in standard English, but the Scots pronunciation *nicht, licht* has preserved the original sounds. It is probably the case, too, that the modern American sound system is nearer to that of Shakespeare than is the pronunciation of standard 'English' English.

Modern English cannot be considered to be merely the language of the English. In America, Australia and other English-speaking countries the language is spoken by five or six times the number of British speakers. Now truly an international tongue, English has become the world's most important language and its largest, in the sense that its lexicon far outweighs that of any other language.

Conclusion

In this chapter I have attempted a brief description of a highly complex phenomenon. I have suggested that language is a form of communication which uses arbitrary symbols. The symbols are patterned, and three distinct systems can be seen operating in language: the sound system, the grammatical system and the semantic system. My account of these systems is sketchy, my objective in describing them being simply to demonstrate that they are there. By presenting some information about the languages of the world, their distribution and their origins, I suggested that languages are paradoxically different but fundamentally alike: they are born of man. Finally, I have conducted you on a lightning tour round the history of *the* language – our English – mainly to show that it did not spring whole from the hand of God: it grew, and it keeps on growing and changing.

CHAPTER 2

The Development of Communicative Competence

Introduction

The acquisition and development of language can be studied in at least four different ways. Firstly, there is the question of how the 'humanness' of language can be explained: how it has happened that a human being can speak. Various theories have been constructed to explain this phenomenon, some in the realm of philosophy, some in psychology and some in anthropology. Secondly there is the study of how language skills are developed in children. This is the realm of developmental psychology and – where the study focuses particularly on language learning – the comparatively new science of psycholinguistics. Thirdly, there is the study of the relationship between the developing linguistic powers of children and their mastery of other kinds of behaviour as social beings: this is the preserve of the science of sociology and – where language is the main object of study – sociolinguistics. Finally, there is the study of how children's 'natural' learning processes interact with direct teaching by parents and teachers and how that learning can best be contrived and controlled. This is the realm of pedagogics. The term *pedagogical linguistics* might be applied to the growing volume of studies which deal with aspects of language learning and language teaching. All these disciplines interweave with one another, and many other subjects (such as biology, physiology, communication theory, social anthropology and so on) have valuable contributions to make to scholars' insights into the problems of language development. A massive literature has accumulated on the subject over the last half-century. Most of this is highly speculative and technical and is of little interest to the majority of parents and teachers who, after all, want to know only what is needed to help their own youngsters to develop effective competencies. But an understanding of the theoretical background and some knowledge of the findings of research will provide both reassurance and guidance in the practical matter of helping children to develop linguistic competence.

The Theory of Language Acquisition

The most influential language acquisition theories are those propounded by the behaviourist psychologists following B. F. Skinner and those put forward by Noam Chomsky and subsequent scholars working under his influence. It is fashionable to see the debates between the Skinnerian and Chomskyan schools as reflecting the age-old disputes between the 'environmentalists', who attribute learning mainly to influence exerted on the human organism through contact with other people, and the 'mentalists', who attribute learning mainly to the genetic inheritance of the human mind.* This is a facile perception, however, akin to the 'nurture/nature' fallacy by which people make crude oppositions between the influence of environment and inheritance in determining intelligence. The truth is that behaviourist psychologists readily acknowledge the existence of certain innate capacities which promote language acquisition, and Chomskyan linguists certainly do not ignore the crucial role played in language acquisition by features of the child's environment. The question at issue is: to what *extent* is language 'inherited' or merely 'learned'?

According to Skinner in his book, *Verbal Behavior* (1957), language is a set of behaviours built up by means of a constant succession of responses to stimuli applied to the organism (the child). Behavioural psychologists have shown that carefully structured learning tasks can be performed successfully by organisms such as rats or pigeons by means of 'operant conditioning'. This involves rewarding a correct response even when it has been made by accident, and 'shaping' behaviour towards correct responses by means of 'reinforcing' successful responses.

Applied to language learning this theory, known as S–R (Stimulus–Response), states that if a child produces any linguistic response deemed appropriate by his mother, teacher or any other caretaker he will be met with a rewarding indication of approval or by a corresponding act showing that the response has been 'correct'. Consequently the child will produce the same response to the same stimulus. The response is reinforced by the reward. If the response is not satisfactory it will not be reinforced, so the child will not make it again.

The S–R learning theory can account for a good deal of the language learning a child goes through. It can explain how a child produces speech and also how he learns to understand speech. It does not, however, tell us anything about how the child's utterances

* Plato's *Cratylus* discusses this topic.

(or responses) came to be made in the first place. When a rat first presses the right bar which 'produces' the pellet, it does so by accident. Are we to believe that some *accidental* utterance or response by the child is at the beginning of the learning process? The behavioural psychologists point to imitation as the source of learning: the mother's rewarding behaviour is a secondary means of reinforcement because the child finds it satisfying to imitate her. According to Skinner, the mother will reinforce responses which at first only approximate to the desired response, and by a series of such reinforcements she will gradually 'shape' the child's behaviour towards the kind of behaviour she regards as 'correct' or 'appropriate'.[7]

The Russian psychologist, Pavlov, showed that a response to one stimulus can be elicited by another, associated, stimulus; his classic example of the dog salivating in response to the ringing of a bell in place of the sight of food is a vivid illustration of this 'contiguity' theory. Learning theorists have adapted this idea to language acquisition. They suggest that a word can operate as a 'mediating' stimulus, producing a response in the absence of the original physical stimulus. Thus, through the mediation of language, all kinds of associations can be built between objects. Children learn what words mean by associating the meanings of known words with new words they are used alongside: for example if a child is told that a library is a house for holding books he will associate *house* and *holding* and *books* to form a concept of the word *library*. Mediation theory can also account for the way a child acquires the ability to produce sentences he has never heard before. Different sets of words are classified grammatically in the child's thinking because they occur in the same place in the framework of an utterance. Thus by hearing such strings as 'See the book', 'See the boy', 'See the train', and so on, the child learns to produce a new utterance by inserting a known word in the slot previously occupied by other known words. In this way, by means of imitation, association, substitution and other devices the child gradually builds up a verbal repertoire which, in time, will constitute the grammar, phonology and lexicon of his mother tongue.

Chomsky's devastating criticisms of Skinner's verbal behaviour theory, along with the many confirmations of the alternative Chomskyan theory produced by researchers during the last twenty years, have made it commonplace to reject the behaviourist position.[8] It is certainly true that the theory fails to account adequately for various known facts about language development, but learning theory must not be ignored altogether, for it has thrown light on many problems of language learning, and it has suggested many valuable teaching techniques. A good deal of successful *teaching* of

Base Component
Rules in the mind for
constructing a basic sentence

↓

Deep Structure
The fundamental unfinished
structure of a sentence: e.g.
The boy + future tense + eat + the cake

national Component
the mind for
ng deep structure
ace structure.

Semantic Component
Rules in the mind for
interpreting the meaning
of the sentence.

↓

ructure
will eat the cake

↓

Semantic Interpretation
(The meaning as expressed
by the hearer.)

Component
nd for
sentence'
of language.

↓

esentation

de the Base Component syntactic, implying that
ct that comes first, the meaning of a sentence
lication of semantic rules to a syntactic base. It
aning and syntax are intertwined, that the deep
tic interpretation are one and the same. Thus
mponent – rules in the mind for generating
ctural frame of a sentence and its meaning –
Base Component in my model as the point

sed model which derives from 'Generative

language can be satisfactorily explained by S–R theory, even if its explanation of language *learning* is demonstrably weak.

Chomsky and his elaborators have shown that the behaviourist learning theory is simply unable to account for language acquisition in a satisfactory way. Imitation cannot be held to account for the *source* of utterances. The variety of possible sentences in a child's repertoire is so great, and the number of 'admissible word combinations' is so huge, that no child could learn them all. It is virtually self-evident that any child can produce sentences which are entirely new and original, and that he can make use of all sorts of rules of syntax, morphology and semantics without having been specially taught them. The suggestion that a child learns to make novel sentences by means of slot-filling is also demonstrably inadequate. As Chomsky pointed out, this theory cannot account for the child's ability to use the correct verb in such 'homonymous' constructions as 'Flying kites is fun' and 'Flying monkeys are fun', or his ability to extract the contextually appropriate meaning from an ambiguous sentence such as 'Are you ready to eat'?

Chomsky also pointed out that the information a child gets from his environment is limited in amount, and it is fragmentary and imperfect. This has been confirmed by researchers who have shown that parents tend to 'reward' by approval utterances which may be incorrect grammatically but correct semantically. This ought to have the effect, if the behaviourist theory is valid, of reinforcing ungrammatical sentence constructions. But of course children *do* learn to speak despite the inadequate experience they get from their environment. They learn this fantastically complex ability when they are only a few years old, before they have the intellectual capacity to reason out rules from the inchoate and diffuse data that confront them.

Chomsky points out that this ability to acquire language is obviously not dependent, except marginally, on the child's intelligence or on motivation. Stupid children as well as intelligent ones learn to speak, as do lazy, unmotivated children. No formal teaching is needed. The fact that all normal children acquire their mother tongue with remarkable rapidity suggests, argues Chomsky, that human beings are somehow specially designed to do this.[9]

Chomsky postulates a genetically endowed 'Language Acquisition Device' possessed by all humans. Every child is born with a capacity for language programmed into his brain: an innate 'universal grammar' which enables him to perceive the 'grammaticality' or acceptability of a sentence. This *faculté de langage* consists, he suggests, of a knowledge of 'rules' that relate sound and meaning in a particular way. It is these rules which explain the 'creativity' of *homo loquens* –

his ability to generate an infinite number of new sentences. For Chomsky, a grammar is a set of rules able to account for all the grammatical (that is, *not ungrammatical*) sentences which it is possible to produce in a language. His grammatical model must therefore be described if his theory of language acquisition is to be understood.

The Chomskyan grammar specifies the rules required for constructing sentences. In the mind, the morphemes and words of a sentence are arranged in functional constituents such as subject, predicate, object and so on, and a speaker's knowledge of this internal structure can be represented (in part) by means of *phrase structure* rules. The first of these rules is simply that a sentence (S) can consist of a noun phrase (NP) followed by a verb phrase (VP), and this rule is represented thus:

$$S \rightarrow NP + VP$$

(The arrow is an instruction to 'rewrite' the left-hand symbol as the symbols which follow it.)

Other rules tell us that NP and VP can be 'unpacked' into constituents; thus NP can be rewritten as *Art + N* (article plus noun), and VP can be rewritten as *Aux + V* (auxiliary plus verb). *Art* can be rewritten as *a, an* or *the; Aux* can be rewritten as *can, may, will, should* and so on – all of the items in the closed system of auxiliary verbs in the language.

We can now list some phrase structure rules:

Rule 1 S → NP + VP
Rule 2 NP → Art + N
Rule 3 VP → Aux + V + NP
Rule 4 Aux → (*can, may, will, should, etc.*)
Rule 5 V → (*walk, hit, eat, explain, etc.*)
Rule 6 Art → *a, an, the*
Rule 7 N → (*boy, table, Smith, cake, etc.*)

This very simple grammar will generate sentences like 'The something can or will or may or should something the something'. We can now construct a *derivation* of a sentence. For example, the sentence *The boy will eat the cake* can be derived as follows:

S
NP + VP (by Rule 1)
Art + N + VP (by Rule 2)
Art + N + Aux + V + NP (by Rule 3)
Art + N + Aux + V + Art + N (by Rule 2)
the   boy   will eat   the   cake (by Rules 4, 5, 6, 7)

This derivation can be represented by a tree

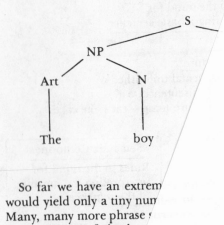

So far we have an extrem
would yield only a tiny num
Many, many more phrase
the sentences of the lan
phrase structure rules a
partial grammar to acco
tion to phrase structu
transform phrase ma
deleting, or rearrang
structure' of a sente
structure into th
mational rules: f
for rearranging
sentences *Boys*
of much the s
account for
Several diffe
into this 's
way she co

This i
Chomsk
morphe
phon
vert
com
th
m

Transfor
Rules i
converti
into surf

Surface St
e.g. *The bo*

Phonological
Rules in the m
converting the
into the sounds

Phonological Repr

Initially Chomsky ma
it is the word-constr
emerging from the ap
is now argued that me
structure and the sema
there is a Semantic Co
simultaneously the stru
which would replace the
of origin of a sentence.
Thus we have the revi
Semantic' theory:

SEMANTIC COMPONENT
Rules in the mind for generating
both the basic sentence and its
meaning.

↓

Semantic Representation
The basic thought which generates
the sentence, e.g. 'I say to you
that in the future something will
happen; the boy will do something;
the cake was eaten; the cake is the
focus of the thought.'

↓

TRANSFORMATIONAL COMPONENT
Rules in the mind for putting the
semantic representation into final
sentence (syntactic) form.

↓

FINISHED SENTENCE
The cake was eaten by the boy

PHONOLOGICAL COMPONENT   MORPHOGRAPHEMIC COMPONENT

↓   ↓

PHONOLOGICAL REPRESENTATION   GRAPHIC REPRESENTATION
Tha kak woz et'n bi tha boi   (The written sentence.)

This, then, is the theory of language emergence which is most
adhered to today. It has no demonstrable psychological reality, nor
does it lay claim to any: it is a powerful conceptual frame into which
we can place many useful hypotheses connecting different aspects of
linguistic and psychological studies. Almost all the most vigorous of
research projects into language development, both in psycholinguistics and in sociolinguistics, begin from theoretical assumptions derived from Chomskyan propositions.

Learning to Speak

We come into this world naked and alone, unable to stand or walk, unable to see clearly or to interpret our surroundings – above all, unable to speak. The very name we give to the preliterate child, *infant*, comes from the Latin *infans*, 'unable to speak'. The absence of speech is one of the most salient characteristics of infancy. And yet the infant is not helpless. He cannot control his sphincter muscles, but he can cry and he has (normally) an assiduous, attentive caretaker over whom he exerts a powerful sway. He can yell and whine and gurgle and babble, and his mother pays close attention to the signs of his strong instinctive drive towards the communication of his needs.

The human child's language capacity develops alongside his maturing control of other forms of behaviour, such as moving his limbs and learning to chew and swallow sustenance. Linguistically, he develops receptive and productive skills at different paces, the receptive (listening and understanding) growing ahead of the productive. At about six weeks, while he is still only gurgling and cooing, he begins to distinguish the sound of his caretakers' voices from all other surrounding noise. At about six months he begins to respond to different tones and pitches of voice, 'recognizing' anger or love; and at this time he has entered the productive phase characterized by 'babbling', which is uttering consonant-and-vowel strings which *sound* like speech – so many fond parents all over the world have heard *mama, papa, dada* and taken them to mean themselves! Between six and nine months he will learn to respond to one or two favourite words, and he may begin to utter some sounds deliberately to convey his need for attention. By about twelve months he is crawling around or even toddling with help, and able to understand a few commands. (Of course, normal children can differ greatly in their speed of growing.)

It used to be thought that in his babbling a child rehearses all the possible sounds the human voice is capable of making, and that he 'acquires' the phonemes of his mother tongue in the way a sculptor creates an artefact, by shedding bits that are of no value. This attractive theory is not now prevalent, but it is true that a baby's babbling is often rich in experimental sounds and includes phonemes that are not employed in the parents' mother tongue. Babies of very different speech communities would seem, however, to utter different kinds of babbling. As a child matures, his babbling takes on more and more of the vocal habits of the language community in which he lives: for example a Chinese baby's babbling will exhibit tonal variety not evident in, say, the babbling of a German baby.

At about nine months the child will begin to repeat the same sounds and to imitate the intonation patterns of his caretakers, so that his babbling sounds elusively like speech. His repetitions (or *reduplications* as they are tehcnically known) may be accompanied by imitations uncannily near to real speech: this stage is often called the *echoic* phase. This, however, is *not* speech. The child is not using sounds as symbols: there is nothing specifically intentional in his speech behaviour. At about twelve months he begins to use single words. These single-word utterances, known as *holophrases*, are usually complete thoughts in the sense that they convey the same burden of meaning that a multiple-word sentence can convey. During the second year of his life the normal child will invent holophrastic utterances of his own to stand for all kinds of objects, persons and actions. This jargon may communicate quite complex messages with great economy of effort. All parents have fond memories of endearing baby-talk such as '*dinkums*' for any drink, water or food or 'gee-gee' for any big animal. A child's jargon will emerge from and reflect his actual environment, and it may change from one generation to another. The word *choo-choo*, for instance, would seem to have disappeared now that trains do not make that noise. During his play, the child will vocalize experimentally, stringing jargon together in long stretches of tone-and-stress-patterned sound. As he matures, the jargon will gradually approximate to genuine speech.[11]

The next stage, towards the end of his second year, is the beginning of the crucially important 'learning explosion' that occurs in the life of every normal child. This is the time he begins to employ two-word utterances and to exhibit the use of grammar. By this time he is *receptively* making use of grammar, since he can respond to fairly complicated commands, questions and statements which would not be comprehensible to him unless he could mentally 'unpack' the sentence structure. By uttering two-word sentences, however, he is beginning to use language creatively. One common type of utterance at this stage is a pattern of what are called 'pivot' words and 'open' class words. In the pivot category are words like *allgone, see, take,* used in the initial position. For example:

Allgone porridge
Allgone Daddy
See Mummy
See shoe
Take shoe

and so on. There can be strings with the pivot in the end position:

Man come
Daddy come
Cup gone
Shoe gone

And there can be longer strings consisting of three or more words with a pivotal structure:

This Mummy red car
That my little dolly
Where my Daddy go?

By the time the child is uttering sentences of this kind – from two to two and a half years – he will have a productive vocabulary of several hundred words and a very much larger receptive vocabulary. He will use language during all his activities, accompanying all his play with talk, replacing his own jargon more and more with genuine speech.[12]

Between the ages of two and a half and five the child will make huge strides in his acquisition of language. At about three years (or before if he is an early developer), he will begin 'filling in' the fabric of his sentences, using the copula (*am, is* etc.), the articles *a, the*, plural forms, auxiliary verbs, tense forms and so on. By the time he is four, the normal child will have acquired a sufficient control of grammar to allow him to communicate adequately for his own everyday purposes. He will have acquired *communicative competence*, the basic linguistic ability to speak which is possessed by all speakers of all natural languages. What remains for him to learn is an easier command of the rules of syntax and morphology, a greater familiarity with the variety of registers* available to him and, of course, the scholastic skills of reading and writing. By the age of about ten (or at puberty) he will have completed his language learning for all practical, everyday purposes. He will continue to perfect his command of English so long as he reads and writes, and of course he will go on increasing his personal lexical store until senility encroaches on his memory. But the all-important linguistic foundations will have been completed by the time he leaves the primary school. If he is going to be a well-educated person, the basic tools for his learning will have been perfected in his first ten years of life.

Educational Disadvantage

Children differ, sometimes remarkably, in the pace at which they develop communicative competence. Even in the same family children will reach a given stage of maturity at different ages. This is quite normal. But children also differ in their *ability to learn*. Some may be superior to others in the number of words and morphemes they can string together in an utterance. Others may be superior in the quality of their utterances, for example using more semantically

* A register is a style of address suitable for a particular situation (see Chapter 5).

complex vocabulary. At any given age, and at any given stage, it is possible to detect different degrees of proficiency in any group of children. It is very difficult, however, to show what it is that makes one child 'cleverer' or 'more intelligent' than another. Intelligence tests, properly administered, will give broad indications of brightness or dullness, but there are no tests of proven value for children under four. Language is so complex a phenomenon, so closely bound up with the individual's personality and with the specific situation in which it is used, that we can hardly ever tell whether a child is performing badly *in his speech* or perversely *in his behaviour*. Controlled observation of children's language is notoriously difficult to achieve, and the data accumulated is extremely hard to analyze. It is therefore wise to ignore the question of how 'intelligent' an individual child may be unless there are indications of real disability.

Children with profound handicap reveal their disability only too clearly when they are born or soon afterwards. Mild forms of handicap, however, may not manifest themselves until it becomes plain that a particular stage of development has not been reached at anything like the right time. All normal children develop stage by stage, achieving the same skills in the same order at roughly the same age. A child suffering some kind of handicap may develop in a less smooth sequence and may spend periods of months on end without showing much sign of moving on to the next stage. Parents should trust their own instincts: if they suspect that something is not quite right about a child they should speak to their doctor or health visitor or nursery teacher.

The environment in which a child spends the formative first five years of life will have a profound effect on his linguistic competence. Language skills develop alongside, and in association with, the development of other abilities, such as the capacity to think out problems and attain goals and the capacity to project the imagination into unknown situations. Even in the same family different children will display markedly different degrees of ability or preference in these respects. While linguistic and intellectual abilities are closely related, it does not follow that the quiet laconic child is necessarily less able than the chatterbox. At the same time, all children use language, as we all do, as an instrument of communication and self-expression; and to an important extent a child will indicate his ability to cope with life by means of language.

Children go to school at the age of five with different personal 'packages' of past experience, preferences, tastes, habits of thinking. All normal children at this age have acquired the basic communicative competence which is 'species specific' in the sense that it is a normal accompaniment of being human. They differ, however, in the ways they use language: in accent, vocabulary, grammatical patterns, and so on. Children from different parts of the English-speaking world will have acquired different dialects as their own version of the mother tongue. Dialects differ in habits of phonology, patterns of grammar and vocabulary preferences. Dialectal variation can also be seen within a single country or district, and within a quite small community there can be distinct dialectal variation between speakers of different social status.*

A great mass of research has shown that social background and educational attainment are related: by and large, children from lower socio-economic homes tend to get less out of schooling than do children from middle-class homes. Various theories have been put forward to explain this relationship. One school of thought, now largely discredited, attributed educational disadvantage to the *sheer absence* of language in the poorer homes. Socially deprived mothers, it was suggested, simply fail to talk with their children sufficiently to enable them to develop the basic linguistic skills. Extreme examples of linguistic deprivation were described in the stories of child isolates such as Isabelle and Genie.[13] Isabelle was found in Ohio in the 1930s. She was over six years old and had been 'brought up' by a deaf mute mother. She was almost wholly speechless, but in the next two years, under care, she quickly developed the normal competence of an eight-year-old. Genie was born in 1957 and when found at the age of thirteen she had been so badly looked after that she could scarcely speak at all. Under care, she developed the basic linguistic skills very slowly. Children brought up under such unnatural conditions are fortunately exceptional, but many believe that similar, though less serious, deprivation is widespread among the very poor. In every industrial society there are people whose economic circumstances are such that their children are socially neglected: the mother is too harassed by work and worry to play and talk with her baby; there may be no father, or only a man who takes no interest in the children; there may be so many children living in such overcrowded conditions that life is a continuous struggle for social identity. This is a bleak picture, frequently exaggerated. But certainly there are groups of families where socio-economic depression is the root cause of cultural deprivation: recent immigrants to industrial societies (especially those with a foreign mother tongue); social inadequates struggling to survive in slums; single-parent families squatting in derelict streets or living precariously in housing schemes. The disad-

* Dialects are discussed in Chapter 5.

vantage the children suffer, however, cannot be described as *linguistic* deprivation. They all acquire basic communicative competence in their mother tongue. Even immigrant non-English-speaking children learn to speak well enough to cope with their immediate environment. They suffer from *cultural* deprivation, but only in the sense that the culture they assimilate is not the same as the culture they are expected to operate within at school.

Another and more persuasive theory is that educational disadvantage stems from differences in the way that people *use* language. The most notable theorist in this field is the sociologist Basil Bernstein, whose work on the relationship between social class and language use has been widely influential.[14] In an early paper Bernstein distinguished between what he called 'public' language use and 'formal' language use. He suggested that the 'public' (later called *restricted*) code is characterized by the choice of 'simple', unelaborate syntax, and often grammatically incomplete sentences. It uses conjunctions such as *so, then, because* repetitively, and it has a rigid and limited use of adjectives and adverbs. Above all, it is 'a language of implicit meaning'. That is to say, the user of a restricted code relies on the other person's shared understanding of the situation in which the exchange occurs. The 'formal' (later called *elaborated*) code is characterized by grammatically complex sentences, the frequent use of prepositions and personal pronouns, a greater range of adjectives and adverbs, and above all more explicitness of meaning. Bernstein emphasizes that children of all social classes have access to both public and formal language codes, but he suggests that working-class children are likely to be restricted to the public code while middle-class children are able to employ either code according to the social context. Working-class children are trapped in a restricted range of language uses. Since the language of schooling is in the elaborated code – the language of formal communication, information, reflection – the working-class child is educationally at a disadvantage when he comes to school.

The ideas of Bernstein and other sociolinguists working in this field have been much misunderstood. It is clear that the language of lower-class children is not intrinsically different from the language of middle-class children. What is different – and it is this that puts the lower-class child at a disadvantage – is the ways in which mothers from different backgrounds use language in communicating with their children. The middle-class mother is 'education-conscious': she will actively teach her child, give him problems to work at, help him to solve them by offering suggestions, reinforce his successes with praise, seek for fresh activities to interest him and stimulate his learning. She will ask him questions, tell him about the world, give him reasoned, patiently elaborated explanations, and let him work at a task at his own pace. All of this helps him to develop what Jerome Bruner calls 'analytic' competence; the use of language as an instrument of thought.

The under-privileged child may not have this nourishing environment. However much he is loved, his mother will be unlikely to have either the time to care for him educationally or the awareness that this is crucially important for his future. As Bruner puts it:

> Poverty, by its production of a sense of powerlessness, alters goal striving and problem solving in those it affects, whether the powerlessness occurs in a depressed London working-class borough, among Kurdistani immigrants to Israel, in a bleak ghetto, among uneducated and abandoned Greenland Eskimo mothers down-and-out in literate Copenhagen, or in the midst of Appalachia.[15]

But it would be a grave mistake to ascribe these disadvantages to all working-class children. They are a consequence of poverty, of the restrictions, harassments and worries of living in overcrowded homes in circumstances where the exigencies of making ends meet push aside the niceties of playing and teaching and cultivating the sensibilities. Most ordinary working-class homes are by no means deprived, and the children are by no means disadvantaged. They could, however, be more *advantaged* if their parents could give more time and thought to the conscious development of their language skills.

Language and Thinking

As we have seen, the behaviourists' 'imitative model' of language development is unsatisfactory mainly because it perceives the child as a passive organism which assimilates linguistic data, whereas there is ample evidence to suggest that the child actively constructs his language systems in interaction with his environment. Chomsky's alternative and more satisfactory explanation presupposes innate learning structures, and this view is strongly supported by the work of Jean Piaget, the world's greatest developmental psychologist. Piaget's theory of cognitive development is extensive and complex, and a brief explanation of it carries the risk of oversimplification. Nevertheless, even a sketchy picture of the Piagetian theory will be useful as a foundation for an understanding of the relationship between language and thinking.[16]

Piaget views learning as resulting from genetically endowed 'functional invariants', which are general organizational characteristics of the human mind. These include the processes of *assimilation* and *accommodation*. The process of assimilation constitutes the organism's efforts to incorporate any new stimulus into its own existing structures: an example is that because a baby instinctively sucks the nipple he will suck someone's finger using the same *schema* or pattern of behaviour. The process of *accommodation* constitutes the organism's efforts to adapt its behaviour to the environment: thus the assimilatory behaviour involved in picking up an object within reach will become the accommodatory behaviour of crawling along the floor to pick up a more distant object. Learning involves both processes. The child's development proceeds through a continuous process of assimilating new experience and accommodating himself to experience; though continuous, the process of development can be seen to stabilize at times into stages; at each stage there will be repetition of previous processes but also a steady drive towards a higher level of organization. Each stage is the foundation for the succeeding stage.

From birth to about eighteen months the child is in the *sensori-motor* period, when he is coming to terms with his physical environment. In this period his reflexes develop into *schemas* which can be employed to solve simple practical problems such as using a stick to push or pull something. In this stage the child moves from being wholly egocentric towards some consciousness of himself in relation to other people and objects. People do not disappear when they leave a room; toys remain in existence though they have been dropped from the cot.

Between the ages of two and eleven the child is in the *concrete operational* period. Until about the age of seven there is a 'preoperational' phase. An operation is an internalized action, originating from sensori-motor acts such as combining and ordering things. It is an activity in the brain. During the preoperational stage the child learns to internalize concrete features of the world so that later he can employ them symbolically. He can explore symbolic activity in his play, for example by using a stick for a gun or a cardboard box for a car. In the concrete operational stage he learns to deal in abstractions, ordering things, classifying, making deductions and so on – but still thinking about things as physical objects, working with *concrete operations*.

In the *formal operational* period, from eleven or twelve onwards, the human being is able to use his reason, to operate with logic, to reflect, hypothetize, theorize. This is the last stage in the development of learning structures. Having reached the formal operational period the human being can think logically and creatively. He will go on learning as he matures, but there are no further qualitative changes to occur in his cognitive equipment. Applied to language learning, Piaget's theory of cognitive development provides us with powerful insights. At each stage the child's reaction to new linguistic experience is governed by the knowledge and skills he already has. He interprets and applies new information in terms of what he already knows: he assimilates and accommodates language substance as he encounters it. Language development proceeds through the interaction of experimentation by the child and the internalized cognitive structures he possesses at a given stage. According to the Piagetian theories, language development plays an important role in the development of the intellect, but language is only one of the functions which give us the ability to represent something symbolically: drawing, playing and conceiving mental images all constitute alternative ways of conceptualizing. Piaget considers that mental growth occurs inevitably as the child matures; language is an important but separate accompaniment.

On the other hand, the Russian school of psycholinguists, founded by Vygotsky in the 1920s and extensively developed by Luria, regarded language as *the* essential factor in mental growth.[17] It is the interaction of language and situation, they argued, that gives the child the capacity to organize mental activities. Language plays a crucial role in the development of the intellect. Vygotsky maintained that rational, intelligent communication between minds is impossible without speech, and so the growth of a child's thinking ability and the growth of his linguistic competence are both closely related to his social development. The origin of language in man is man's social life.

Vygotsky proposes four phases in which the ability of verbal thinking develops. Firstly there is the 'primitive' or natural stage akin to Piaget's sensori-motor phase. Then comes a stage in which the child learns the grammatical structures but does not as yet understand the logical operations of functional items such as *if, when, because, although*. This, too, is consistent with Piaget's preoperational stage, in which the grammar of speech is learned before the syntax of thought has been developed. Then there is the stage at which external signs and operations are employed: for example, when talking aloud to himself, or counting on his fingers, the child is 'externalizing' processes of thinking. Later, in the fourth stage, these processes occur internally; 'inner speech' and logical memory have been developed. The internalization of speech, at or after the age of seven, leads to the development of higher forms of intellectual activity. Social interaction is essential to this process; the interaction between child and adult encourages the growth of intellect.

Jerome S. Bruner's work has also contributed valuably to our understanding of the relationship between language and thinking. Bruner suggests that there are three ways in which a person can 'represent' experience and make use of it. *Enactive* representation works through action – learning physical responses and habits in learning to ride a bicycle or play tennis. *Iconic* representation depends on visual organization (or by means of the other senses) – it works through perceiving patterns and making use of them. *Symbolic* representation uses language – we translate experience into language and by means of words we can form hypotheses and solve problems without direct recourse to actual things or events.

Intellectual development, says Bruner, 'seems to run the course of these three systems of representation until the human being is able to command all three'.[18] These stages, reminiscent of the Piagetian periods of sensori-motor, concrete-operational and formal-operational growth, are accompanied by appropriate types of mental need. Bruner argues that learning depends on the opportunities provided to allow the child to explore his environment in terms of his own needs and capacities, and so we must encourage 'discovery learning', leading the child to find out for himself. Bruner uses the notion of *compatibility*, which appears to contain echoes of Piaget's notions of assimilation and accommodation: new knowledge will only be truly possessed by a child when it has been connected with his existing repertoire of ideas. The 'channelling capacity', that is the ability to handle information, can be improved when information is organized by the teacher. Discovery learning helps the child to develop the ability to devise strategies for solving problems and for obtaining new much-needed information. The way in which the child structures his learning in a given lesson or activity will help his understanding of regularities and relationships in other situations. Bruner conceives this structuring process as an ability to 'code' information. Language enables us to codify the input of our senses and thus to make sense of our experience. The coding ability of the human mind allows us to create and to comprehend meaningful language out of all the raw linguistic substance we encounter.

Bruner proposes the term 'species minimum' for the basic linguistic competence possessed by all speakers of all natural languages. Beyond this basic competence there is 'communicative competence', which includes the ability to use language for everyday purposes within ordinary contexts. Communicative competence is also 'species minimum' in the sense that every normal person can be expected to acquire it without special training. Communicative competence, says Bruner, can be taken to involve the achievement of the 'concrete operations' described by Piagetian psychologists. Beyond this species-minimal competence there is what Bruner calls 'analytic competence'. Analytic competence (like Piaget's 'formal operations') involves intellectual activity: 'the prolonged operation of thought processes exclusively on linguistic representations, on propositional structures, accompanied by strategies of thought and problem solving appropriate not to direct experience with objects and events but with ensembles of propositions'.[19]

Analytic competence, then, is the ability to use language for thinking. It is not acquired naturally. It must be developed through education; that is, through being engaged in structured learning activities. The mental skills involved in the higher-order uses of language are not acquired without the intervention of an educator. The educator during the child's early years is usually the mother, assisted (or sometimes replaced) by other people concerned with the child. The play-school group leaders, the nursery schoolteacher, anyone who contributes to the growth of language skills, are also contributing to the growth of educational potentiality, the readiness of the child to learn more. That some children have greater educational potential than others is partly a consequence of their inherited predispositions and capacities. But it is also a consequence, in large measure, of the knowledge and educative skills and motivation of the parents and teachers they have the good fortune to live with during these crucially important years of growth.

Helping Children to Develop Competence

The most important way in which parents and others can help the preschool child to develop linguistic skills is to make sure he has ample opportunities for play. The functional value of play has long been recognized as a factor in language development. Infants play with language almost from the beginning. Ruth Weir, in her book, *Language in the Crib*, tells how her son Anthony, at the age of one and a half lying in his cot after the light was out, played with words, rehearsing phrases heard during the day.[20] As he plays alone with toys, the young child uses language in various ways. In his so-called 'egocentric' speech the child gives a running commentary, as it were, of what he is doing, describing each action or reacting verbally to the little crises he enacts. For example:

'Car goes 'long street – oh no! – (as it bumps into something) – Come *on*, Tony! – little red car, *big* red car'. . .

When playing with other children, he may use language for directing others: 'Put yours *there* – no, *there*, silly! – Be careful!' and so on. Often, during such play the child's speech may be primarily egocentric, paying little or no attention to the other children. Yet the very presence of others will promote the production of speech; so the company of other children during play is an aid to development.

Children, like adults, are more persevering when playing than they are when under pressure to perform duties. The absence of pressure helps them to resist frustration, so they give up less readily. Play is therefore a fruitful source of language learning. What the psychologists call 'symbolic activity' – the use of events or objects to stand for other things – can be indulged in freely during play. This helps the child to experiment, trying out newly learned words and phrases and different language functions such as instructing, questioning, and so on. Playing together generates interactivity and 'rules' of behaviour that resemble and reinforce the signals and responses of linguistic communication. In play, too, children can indulge their love of imitating others.

The 'education-oriented' mother will work hard at providing play opportunities for her child, knowing that it has a high educational value. She will also pay attention to her child while he plays, even when she has time only to keep a casual eye on him. She will be ready to offer a bit of guidance, or a word of comfort or approval. She will play with her child as often as she can, taking advantage of opportunities as they arise to answer questions, encourage imitation, expand or extend his utterances, and match the complexity and style of her own speech to his. All of these processes – *imitation, expansion, extension* and *matching* – are known factors in the promotion of language learning.

Imitation

This is a valuable source of learning for the young child. Between the ages of two and five – the 'learning explosion' period – he will delight in imitating the speech of others, especially of course that of his parents and siblings. He will practise speech routines while he plays. He will echo some phrases that takes his fancy, often loudly and repetitively. He will copy adults' habits, such as question tags – *aren't I?, isn't it?, won't he?* – sometimes using them indiscriminately and sometimes producing entertaining ineptitudes.

The younger child will not imitate exactly, rather he will reduce the imitated form so that it fits the level of complexity his own grammar has reached. Thus the adult's sentence 'It's cold outside so we'll stay indoors' might be remodelled by the child as 'Cold outside, stay doors'. Many a mother will earnestly try to correct the 'faulty' grammar of her child, not knowing that he has not yet reached the stage of being able to employ the 'correct' (adult) grammar. During the years of 'child grammar' the child will not even *hear* the adult pattern. David McNeil reports the following exchange:

Child: Nobody don't like me.
Mother: No, say 'Nobody likes me'.
Child: Nobody don't like me.

This went on until the child had responded in the same way *eight times!* Then the dialogue developed:

Mother: No, listen carefully, say 'Nobody likes me'.
Child: Oh, nobody don't likes me.[21]

Many researchers have confirmed that explicit correction of this kind has no beneficial effect whatsoever on the child's development. So long as he is in a given stage of linguistic maturation, any child will be 'trapped' within the limits of competence appropriate to that stage.

This is dramatically demonstrated by the two-word 'pivot plus open class' grammar I have already described (pp. 29–30) and also by the phenomenon of 'the over-generalized rule'. This is seen during a phase when the child has learned to use the past tense *-ed* ending for verbs. Having learned to say 'I painted' or 'He played' and so on, he will also say 'I goed', 'He maked' and so on even when he may have been using correct forms such as *went* and *made* for some time. This phase cannot be accounted for by the child's exposure to adult models; it must be simply that he has begun to perceive the rule for forming regular past tenses and applies it indiscriminately. He is at a stage when he avoids exceptions. In a succeeding phase he will perceive that there is one rule for one set of verbs and another rule for another set of verbs. During this phase of avoiding exceptions he will apply the same kind of 'uniformity' to syntax. Thus he will misinterpret sentences like 'Mum promised Dad to buy that' because it does not conform to the 'rule' exemplified by a sentence like 'Mum told Dad to buy that', or 'Mum wanted Dad to buy that'.

Expansion and Extension

The mother or other caregiving adult will reinforce the child's learning more constructively by using the techniques known as *expansion* and *extension*. Expansion can be illustrated thus:

Child: The man goed into the house.
Mother: Oh yes, that's right, the man went into the house.
Child: Then he breaked a window.
Mother: He broke *two* windows, didn't he?

By expanding the child's utterance the mother seems to be continuing the dialogue without paying irritating attention to the errors. At the same time she is presenting a correct model for the child to imitate. Although it is true that the child will not adopt the correct form until he has reached the state of readiness to learn the next rules in the game, he must reach that stage at *some* time, and he may reach it sooner if he has ample data to imitate. However, it is much more natural that a parent should respond to *what* the child says rather than *how* he says it. When this happens the parent is using the technique of *extension:*

Child: The man goed into the house.
Mother: Yes, and it was all dark, wasn't it?
Child: And he breaked a window.
Mother: What with, do you remember?

Here the dialogue proceeds without the interruption of corrections or even expansions, which may occasionally be conspicuous enough to detract from the naturalness of the talk. It is possible, of course, to combine expansions and extensions, and this will do no harm so long as the dialogue proceeds at a friendly pace.

Matching

But it would be a mistake for a parent or teacher to work too deliberately to apply the 'techniques' in their dialogues with children. The important thing is to remember that the correction of faulty grammar or vocabulary is not a productive activity. It is much more valuable to enter into a creative exchange of ideas and impressions which will engage the child's active imaginative capacity for using language. This is where *matching* is most important. Obviously the adult cannot address a three or four year-old child as if he were fully grown. Parents intuitively use simpler syntax and familiar vocabulary when talking with their children, and it is important to engage in dialogue that the child is capable of sustaining. This does not mean that 'baby-talk' is appropriate. Obviously language habits that the child has outgrown would be as poor a match as would language he cannot comprehend. The art of talking helpfully with a child lies simply in knowing him and treating him as the unique personality he is, being interested in him and sharing his interests and establishing a warm, natural relationship that allows you to help him explore the magic realms of the language you share.

The well-run nursery class is the most supportive and helpful of environments for the child of three to five. The teachers are professionally trained to provide structured play conditions designed to promote learning, not only of language but of other aspects of maturation such as the control of the body, the understanding of number, the perception of space and so on. The nursery curriculum in the past has been thought to lay too much emphasis on uncontrolled play, and too little emphasis on specific activities to promote language competence. Nowadays this deficiency has been rectified, and teachers are trained to use various professional strategies for language development.

Among these strategies is the provision of opportunities for the children to *hear* language being used creatively and to use it productively themselves. Thus the teacher will tell the children stories, encouraging them to predict the outcomes or participate in the many repetitive sound patterns a good story will contain. She will deliberately read a story to them regularly, so that they come to know that books can offer these pleasurable experiences. She will engage them in role-playing (being the postman, policeman, nurse or other familiar 'stranger') and show them how people use English for different reasons and to do different jobs. She will conduct singing and dancing and mime to help them express themselves joyously in their mother tongue. She will engage them in dialogue while performing tasks such as putting on clothes, cutting out shapes, making things with clay or dough.

All of these strategies can, of course, be used at home or at play-school by parents. To be brought up well in respect of language competence the child should be amply provided with the experience of using language receptively (by listening) or productively (by speaking or singing). Experience should also be comprehensive: that is, the various functions of language need to be explored and practised.

Various categorizations of language functions have been proposed. One researcher suggests nine 'primitive speech acts' in very young children. These are labelling, repeating, answering, requesting action, requesting an answer, calling, greeting, protesting, practising.[22] M. A. K. Halliday proposes six functions:

1. *Instrumental* This is the simplest model, the use of language as 'a means of getting things done', for the satisfaction of personal material needs, serving the 'I want' function.

2. *Regulatory*   The use of language as a means of regulating the behaviour of others, serving the function of 'Do as I tell you'.

3. *Interactional*   This model refers to the use of language for maintaining and mediating one's relationships with others, serving the 'me and him' (or 'me and Mummy') function.

4. *Personal*   This is the model which enables the child to express his own individuality, serving the 'Here I come' function.

5. *Heuristic*   This model refers to language as a means of finding out, questioning, serving the function 'Tell me why'.

6. *Imaginative*   This model enables the child to project himself into an environment of his own making, to create a world of make-believe, serving the 'Let's pretend' function.[23]

These are not models of language acquisition, nor are they psychological or pedagogical categories; they are merely some of the functions language can perform, ways in which children can be seen to operate with language. In another sense, they are illustrations of the great variety of the uses of language, and for the educator this is the chief importance of Halliday's analysis. Teachers ought to be aware of the many ways in which language is used in social intercourse and in the course of the individual's life. Again, recalling the work of Piaget and Bruner, we must realize the importance of founding teaching procedures on the child's existing knowledge and experience, enabling him to make new experience compatible with what he already knows.

A language function which is not seen in the behaviour of younger children is that which Halliday calls *representational* – the use of language to convey information and express propositions. This is a sophisticated ability which is developed through education. Joan Tough has created a systematic pattern of learning strategies by means of which the child can be helped to develop this and other functions related to the abilities needed for analytic competence. She distinguishes four functions, each of which is characterized by a use of language to achieve a certain purpose. The *directive* function is concerned with directing actions, of oneself or of others. The *interpretative* function is concerned with experiences and communication about them. The *projective* function involves thinking about experiences not tied to immediate circumstances: this is using the imagination to project oneself into the future or into other people's experiences or into fantasy. The *relational* function is concerned with interpersonal relations, communicating and getting on with others. Tough's analysis yields a set of distinctive uses of language, each of which can be shown to develop as the child matures. The interpretative function emerges in three uses of language: *predictive*, as in forecasting or anticipating events; *empathetic*, as in imagining and expressing the feelings of other people; and *imaginative*, as in renaming objects or symbolizing events.[24] All of these uses of language can be promoted in the child's growth by skilled teaching, and Dr Tough and her associates have developed a comprehensive language curriculum for the preschool stage. Because the child-adult dialogue is seen to be the most productive means of cultivating thinking strategies, a range of insights and practices have been devised by which the adult can help the child to internalize the language and thinking skills which make up the competencies needed for successful learning in school.

Conclusion

In this chapter I have sketched various theories of language acquisition and argued that, in some way we do not fully understand as yet, every child is born with the potential capacity to acquire his mother tongue. I have outlined the processes of language learning, stage by stage, showing that the basic communicative competence we all possess comes naturally in a sequence of stages. I have described some of the socio-economic conditions which inhibit the growth of competence, arguing that it is not in *language* but only in the way it is habitually used that some children are deficient. I have described the theories of linguistic and cognitive development which enable us to devise our educational strategies, and I have given an account of various ways in which a child's growth can be helped. In all of this a clear message emerges for the parents and teachers concerned with the preschool child: nature will do most of the job, but you can help by paying attention to the child as an individual, providing the wherewithal for the youngster to look, listen, imitate, explore, experiment and – above all – have fun with language.

CHAPTER 3

The Development of Language Skills

Introduction

It is curious that, despite the fact that the main vehicle of communication is speech, this aspect of language has been much neglected in schools. This is no doubt because very little was known until recently about the speech behaviour of people or about the importance of talk in learning processes. The comparatively new sociolinguistic study called 'Discourse Analysis' is beginning to throw light on the role of speech in social intercourse, and it is now possible to recommend a new emphasis on the use of talk in education.

Reading, on the other hand, has long been a major preoccupation of educators, and thousands of books have been written about teaching reading. The most recent researches have drawn upon psycholinguistic theory, and it has now become apparent that reading is as much a matter of communicative competence as are speech and listening. Other modern areas of research, such as communication theory and the psychology of perception, have thrown light on the actual processes of reading. Teachers are prey to the fashions and gimmicks which abound in the reading field and new 'reading schemes' keep appearing on the market. The truth appears to be, however, that any reasonably competent teacher can teach beginners to decode. After that the development of efficient reading depends on the individual's intelligence, interest in things and knowledge of his mother tongue. There are ways of helping pupils to develop better reading skills, but there are no magic methods.

We know so little about writing that it is not surprising that it is so inadequately taught. What we do know about the psycholinguistics of writing makes it plain that, like speaking, listening and reading, it is most effectively learned through sheer experience of using it. Proficiency depends more on the individual's general linguistic ability than on taught skills. All the same, there is much that a good teacher can do to help the pupil develop mastery of the art of composing on paper. It is possible, too, for the teacher to improve his own writing skills by paying attention to certain features of the process, and of course also by practising the art with zeal and persistence. Robert Louis Stevenson's phrase 'playing the sedulous ape' is probably more apt than even he realized. The simple truth about learning to write good English is that it requires unremitting hard work, preferably under the guidance of a good teacher.

Spelling is a linguistic concomitant of writing, and must be learned. The orthography of English is a fascinating and rewarding study. Among other benefits it confers is the reassurance that English spelling does have rules which can be learned. Two kinds of 'rules' can be explained: firstly, the rules inherent in the behaviour of the English language; and secondly, rules that have been enunciated simply to serve as aids to correct spelling. These 'artificial' rules are best treated as a reference list to be kept (in the mind or, if necessary, on the desk) for use as needed. A minor, though still necessary, concomitant to writing is punctuation. This, too, can be described simply with lists of examples to aid the memory.

Speech, Talk and Listening[25]

The communicative competence with which children are equipped when they begin formal schooling is more than just the knowledge of the language that Chomsky called *competence*. For Chomsky, competence is the basic operational knowledge of grammar that underlies the ideal speaker and listener; *performance* is the actual utterances of a speaker of the language. A similar distinction had been made, many decades earlier, by Ferdinand de Saussure, the great French scholar now acknowledged to be the father of modern linguistics. De Saussure gave the name *langue* to the linguistic system known to all speakers of a particular language, and the name *parole* to the language actually spoken. *Langue* (or *competence*) is a set of abstract rules and data; *parole* (or *performance*) is the realization of these rules in actual utterances.

Communicative competence, however, is the ability to use the mother tongue *in context*, that is in real situations consisting of one or more speakers, one or more listeners, a location, a reason for communicating, and so on – all the real-life influences that bear upon what is called a *speech event*. A speech event occurs within a situation – for example a lesson, or a party, or a game. A situation may consist of one speech event, or it may contain a number of speech events – for example, conversations with different people at a party.

In turn, a speech event consists of one or more *speech acts*. A speech act is a functional unit of oral communication. It may consist of a sentence, or part of a sentence, or merely a word. The meaning of a speech act is not the same as the meaning of the words that comprise it: indeed, a speech act derives its meaning from the *situation* and not from the *grammatical form* of the utterance. A speech act has an 'illocutionary' force over and above its locutionary content. For example, to say 'I promise (something)' is not merely to tell the hearer something: it is *promising*. The utterance is a *performative* event. Again, if I am trying to tell you something, I have succeeded in telling it as soon as you know what it is I am trying to tell you. A speech act, then, is part of a situation in which communication occurs. It may take the form, in English, of a question, or a statement, or a command, or a request. But each of these can be realized by means of a sentence in the interrogative form, or the declarative form or the imperative form. For instance, the sentence *Can you come with me* can be a question, command or request according to the way it occurs in a situation. Again, a command can take any of such forms as:

Can you shut the window? (Question)
It would be nice to have the window shut. (Statement)
Shut the window. (Command)
The window, John! (Question?/Statement?/Command?)
John, dear! (With a gesture) (Question?/Statement?/Command?)

The ability to operate within speech events which are contained in everyday situations is learned easily by normal children. The use of speech is a 'species minimum' in the sense that it is not learned through deliberate teaching, but rather through the ordinary interactions of daily life. Conversing, on the other hand, is the employment of speech acts with a view to exchanging meanings. An important feature of conversation is that utterances are closely related to each other as they occur in sequence. In other words they are related within one speaker's chain of utterances or related by means of speaker–listener responses. By the time they reach school most children will have learned many of the social techniques of conversation, but their ability to *initiate* and *sustain* conversation will vary in accordance with their previous linguistic experience and knowledge. The experience that promotes conversing ability is the activity we call *talk*.

Talk may be defined as *ordered speaking*. It consists of oral exchange about a topic. It involves listening as well as speaking since it is essentially an interactive process engaged in by two or more persons. Talk is extremely important as a vehicle of teaching and learning since no other process has ever even approximated to it as an instrument for the transmission of thought. Even within a peer-group talk is a valuable means whereby children learn the skills of discourse, such as selecting and sustaining a conversational topic, interrupting, denying, acknowledging, agreeing, expanding, extending and matching. All of these skills (and many more) develop from practice. Talk also helps develop the skills that comprise logical thinking. Although we do not know the precise relationship between language and thinking, it is evident that talk enables children to develop strategies for the coordination and transmission of ideas. Talk gives form to their thinking, allowing them to impose upon it sequence and coherence. We may think of language as a *clothing* of thought, but it is better to think of it as the embodiment of thought, just as a melody is the embodiment of the sounds of music. Talk helps children to sort out and recreate their thoughts. We think *in* language and talk helps us to think more effectively. The little girl who, being told to 'Think before you speak' said, 'How do I know what I think until I hear what I say?', expressed an important idea for all educators. 'Speaking your thoughts' is in a real sense the very act of thinking. It is in the verbal teasing out of one's thinking that one learns to think efficiently, and the process of 'talking your way through' a problem is an important learning technique.

Since talk requires one to listen, the skilled teacher will contrive activities with young children which give them a sense of the importance of careful listening. There is much discussion among teachers of 'listening skills', but in fact little is known about the process and it is doubtful whether listening can be separated for teaching purposes from talk. What *is* listening?[26] The ear receives speech in the form of sound-waves. If the hearer knows the language he can extract information from the acoustic substance which enables him somehow to reconstruct the meaning (or an approximation of it) encoded initially by the speaker. The process can be crudely illustrated thus:

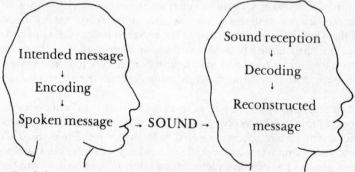

Intended message ↓ Encoding ↓ Spoken message → SOUND → Sound reception ↓ Decoding ↓ Reconstructed message

But it is an extremely complex process, involving a mass of mental and physiological activity. Prior knowledge of the language is essential and so is knowledge (most of it intuitive) of all the constraints and choices which make the language behave in the way it does, for example the rules of sequence which determine what categories of words are 'allowed' to follow given words. If a message is to make sense both the speaker and the hearer must be aware that it makes sense and no message will make sense if the sequence of words are unmeaningful to either. In English, certain sequences are simply not allowed. Thus the utterance *Not is it the* cannot form a message. On the other hand, the sequence *Not is* if uttered by a foreigner would be reconstructed by a native English speaker to mean 'It's not' or some such message. Knowledge of the sequential probabilities in the language helps the listener to predict the continuation of a message. For example, if you establish that a word begins with *ex-* the range of choice for filling the next position is quite wide. If the next position is occupied by *ch* (yielding *exch-*) the possible choices are only two (*e* or *a*) and if you arrive at *exche-* you have no option but to complete the word *exchequer*.[27] Decoding is therefore a process of deciding what a message *is going to be*, or even what a message *ought to have been*. Hence, if there is a conflict between what the actual message is and what the hearer *thinks* the message is *likely to be*, the latter usually wins. Listening is a process of *interpreting* as well as *decoding*. Decoding is the turning of sound into language; interpreting is the turning of language into meaning.

The whole process of listening can be illustrated thus:

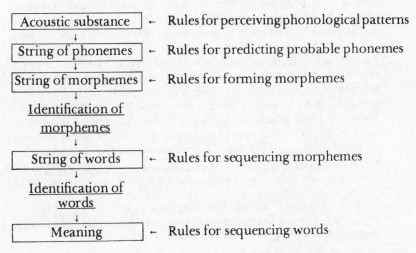

	Application of
Acoustic substance	← Rules for perceiving phonological patterns
↓	
String of phonemes	← Rules for predicting probable phonemes
↓	
String of morphemes	← Rules for forming morphemes
↓	
Identification of morphemes	
↓	
String of words	← Rules for sequencing morphemes
↓	
Identification of words	
↓	
Meaning	← Rules for sequencing words

Intelligent listening, then (as distinct from hearing), depends on general linguistic knowledge. A huge store of linguistic information has to be drawn upon and applied to any given chain of acoustic events if it is to be decoded and comprehended. Anyone possessing basic communicative competence can operate the process, but efficiency will vary with the extent of the store of knowledge available to the listener. The kind of knowledge required for the development of listening ability is the same as that required for the development of all the language skills. That is to say, efficiency in listening, like efficiency in talking, reading and writing, depends on one's knowledge of grammar and vocabulary and one's ability to process linguistic information, which depends, in turn, on one's experience of the way language works.

The situations contrived by the teacher to promote these skills will vary with the age and aptitude of the pupil, but in essence they will all be designed to do the same things. Firstly, each situation will capture the pupil's attention and interest, so that he is ready to work hard at the communication processes. Secondly, the situation will contain – as a groundwork, as it were – known linguistic information or experience. Thirdly, it will provide the pupil with new linguistic knowledge or experience which he can accommodate to his existing store. Whatever the type of skills being taught, the learning will essentially consist of the reception and accommodation of new (or newly identified) language. In practically every instance, moreover, the learning will occur in a context of talk.

For the younger primary school child the teacher capitalizes on his love of play by engaging him in games of various kinds. Naming games such as Kim's Game, I spy, and Lotto* increase his wordhoard and improve his sensitivity to word-object-symbol relationships. Play with pictures, toys and everyday objects leads to the acquisition of categorizing, classifying and contrasting terms. Identikit games,† role-playing, acting out stories and other such activities build up experience of using language to describe, denote, identify objects and persons. Physical games, music and movement, building games, Hunt the Thimble and similar activities help to increase the child's stock of locative terms such as *in, behind, in front of, around* and so on. Dramatic play in the 'Home Corner', acting out stories, sequencing

* *Kim's Game:* identifying which object has been removed from a table.
   I spy: guessing what object a player has in mind – the only clue being the sound of its initial.
   Lotto: collecting and naming items using picture cards.
   † *Identikit* is guessing which clothes fit a doll or figure by listening to your partner's description.

picture-story items and other such activities increase the child's knowledge of relational terms such as *then, after, while, during*; connectives such as *first, next, at last*; and tense-marked verbs. Above all, these activities give children experience of using sentence patterns to suit the speaker's purpose.[28] Perhaps the most important form of play in the primary school is role-playing. Almost all the functions of language can be explored and experimented with in imagined situations where the child draws upon remembered experience and simulates persons and events. This activity can generate a variety of speech events in different situations: situations such as travelling, shopping, telephoning, and so on that involve *explaining, apologizing, complaining, instructing, interrogating, encouraging, coaxing*, to name but a few.

As children mature, and in particular as they reach the stage of learning and developing reading and writing skills, it is important that they should be led to appreciate language as a phenomenon. Knowledge *of* English (that is, the operational knowledge that enables us to use it) needs to be supplemented and enriched by knowledge *about* English (that is, awareness of language as an immensely important aspect of human behaviour, awareness of it as the most potent of all mankind's tools, and awareness of it as a source of endless pleasure). Proficiency in the uses of English can certainly be developed without having much academic knowledge about language, but a love of the language and a sense of how it works must surely be of value. For this reason teachers should encourage thinking *about* language in pupils of all ages. This does not necessitate deliberate teaching of academic facts about English, but it does entail a readiness to draw attention to any feature of the language that emerges in any situation, and a readiness to use and convey the language that is needed to talk about the language.[29] Linguists call this a *metalanguage*. All teachers employ one, whether or not they are conscious of doing so. It is an important element of language-teaching that the teacher should be able to share this metalanguage in such a way that the pupils can profit from knowing it. The best way of teaching pupils the terminology they need for English is simply to mention terms as the need seems to occur. Names like *speech, story, print, book, beginning, ending, chapter, play, character*, and so on are all part of the metalanguage and can easily be taught without explicit reference. Names like *letter, word, sentence, noun, adjective, verb, adverb* and so on may need to be explicated, but they can be used casually at an early stage and explained in greater detail as the need occurs at later stages. It is important that terminology of this sort should occur during talk, and not be confined – in actuality and in the pupil's perceptions – to written language activities.

Talk should be deliberately contrived as a learning context at every stage in schooling. Unfortunately this essential mode of teaching and learning has been, and is still, neglected. It may be that teachers, like most people, take it for granted that children learn by listening alone. It may be simply that it is difficult to arrange dialogue in a classroom containing one adult and a couple of dozen or more lively young-sters. Whatever the reason, the neglect of talk as an educative activity must certainly diminish the successful teaching of all the other language skills. However difficult it may be to contrive, talk should be a planned activity in every classroom.

Teachers should realize that learning is not a necessary concomi-tant to teaching. If I sell you something, you must necessarily buy it – selling and buying are coordinate terms. But teaching and learning are not coordinate terms: I may *teach* intensively, but the pupil may not *learn*. Or it may be that while I teach my pupil is learning something I do not intend him to learn – to dislike me, or the sub-ject, for example. The proper coordinate of teaching may well be simply 'pupilling'.[30]

This disjunction arises from the circumstance that the teaching –learning process consists very largely of the verbal transmission of concepts. The pupil is expected to internalize concepts which have been verbally formulated by the teacher. Some concepts are so com-plex that the teacher needs to use a preliminary sequence of 'leading up' concepts or to present experiences which offer instances (and non-instances) of the concept. All of this can be done verbally in the dyad of teacher and pupil. Efficient teaching, however, must result in perceived learning; and the usual way for a pupil to show that he has grasped a concept is to verbalize it in return, or to say something to indicate that he has accommodated the concept. Spoken responses of this kind, however, are very weak instances of demonstrated learning. Talking about a concept, or about a topic that requires the use of the concept, is not only a good way to demonstrate that it has been learned but also an excellent way of reinforcing it.

Discourse as a teaching device is as old as civilization. It is therefore surprising that the vast resources of our education system have not been employed to devise ways of making talk an essential feature of all teaching. It has been pointed out in recent years that many teachers seem to be so unaware of the role of speech in learning that they expound their special subjects in language which their pupils cannot understand.[31] It is obvious that a pupil who does not know the meaning of terms will not learn the concepts the terms carry. It is all too possible for the teacher to employ unfamiliar terms which will inhibit the pupil's learning. Even when a teacher is aware of this danger he may simply not know how best to convey his information in verbal formulations accessible to the pupil. Such concepts in mathematics as *oppositeness* or *magnitude* may be quite difficult for the pupil to attain without copious experience of instances, and may be very difficult for the teacher to exemplify in a short space of time. Teachers of history or economics may freely use such familiar terms as *state* and *society* without fully realizing that their pupils' understanding of the concepts is vague.* There is, moreover, a kind of bookish, textbook syntax and vocabulary which many teachers use when expounding a subject. This is the 'language of secondary education' which is often quite obscure to many pupils. The employment of talk – the planned use of free oral exchange between teacher and pupil or between pupil and pupil – will give the teacher ample evidence about his pupils' grasp of concepts, and also about the efficacy of his own teaching.

Talk is an important characteristic of the educative home. Parents who encourage (or even *allow*) their children to converse during meals are promoting their language skills. Parents who join in, and manage to engage in discourse that the children attend to, are helping even more. Of course this activity may often degenerate into verbal rioting, but it is part of growing up to learn the discipline needed for conversation. Talk about homework topics, however boring to a busy adult, will yield valuable reinforcement to learning, especially if child and parent manage to reverse the student–teacher role so that the youngster can experience the pleasure of expounding a subject to an interested adult. Children can also be helped by sitting in on conversation with adults, especially if the topics pursued have some connection with their own concerns. Dialogue between a child and a caring adult is perhaps the most fruitful of all language learning, particularly where the adult is skilful enough to 'teach' without being didactic or prosy.

The importance of talk should not obscure the need for a freer use of speech in other ways. Talk is ordered speech, but spontaneous speech also has a function in learning. It is an unfortunate characteristic of schooling that it generally occurs in classrooms where a teacher must demand disciplined behaviour, because it is a natural thing to voice one's thoughts, feelings and needs in the process of learning. Pupils ought to be able to indulge in what Edward Sapir[32]

* Robert N. Sinclair cites the example of an American student who read a passage on European history and then observed, 'England became Protestant, but the French still believed in God and remained Catholic'. ('Sociolinguistics and Reading Comprehension', in *Viewpoints in Teaching & Learning*, Vol. 54, University of Indiana, 1978.)

called 'expressive speech' – the free flow of speech that verbalizes one's thoughts and feelings – so that they can exercise some control on their own learning. Verbal recognition of understanding – for example by exclaiming *Ah-hah!* – is a natural aid to learning, as is the spontaneous demand for the speaker to repeat an utterance or the expression of doubt or hesitation or the asking of questions. All of these speech acts are commonplace in the home or the street or anywhere one person is learning from another, but they are usually forbidden in the classroom. Learning is a two-way process: the pupil should be free to regulate the teacher's behaviour to accommodate his own thought-processes. Many teachers object to this sort of treatment from a pupil though any parent would not only tolerate it but welcome it from his child. Teaching will never be fully efficient until it is possible for pupils to be natural in their learning behaviour in school. Whatever means may be required to make natural speech behaviour possible must be devised. In the primary school, group methods allow these conditions when they are properly managed. Similar conditions ought to be contrived for older pupils, at least for lessons where oral exchange is a prerequisite to learning.

Learning to Read[33]

Reading is a form of communication which resembles the act of communication between speakers. Communicative efficiency, in both cases, depends on the participants' control of the symbols employed. In the speaking-and-listening process, the symbols are vocal and audible and the act of comprehension involves responding to the recurrent and contrastive acoustic features. In reading, the receptive participant must respond to the recurrent and contrastive features of the written language. Just as the listener has learned to associate vocal symbols with meanings, so the reader has learned to derive meaning from a flow of graphic configurations. In both cases, understanding comes from perceiving *distinctive features*. These distinctive features are the crucial distinguishing marks that make one item – a letter, or a word, or a phrase – different from all other items.

A *feature* is a characteristic of a *grapheme*, which is any single meaningful shape used in a writing system. A feature can be common to more than one grapheme: for example, the printed letters *b, d, h,* each has an ascender or upstroke, while the letters *p* and *q* have descenders or downstrokes and the letters *m, n* and *v* have neither. Features are *distinctive* when they enable you to reduce the number of alternatives a grapheme could be. A distinctive feature conveys information about a letter, but may not give you all the information you need to identify a grapheme. For example, the descender of a *p* tells you that this letter is not *a* or *o* but it does not tell you that it is *p* and not *q*; for this you need to notice the feature *b* which, along with the descender marks the letter *p*.

The English alphabet contains twenty-six letters but only five distinctive features are necessary to distinguish all of these letters. Also, when you are able to perceive about a dozen distinctive features in words, you are able to identify a word from among thousands of alternatives. The skilled reader is so adept at perceiving the distinguishing features of printed graphemes that he can identify words even when only some of the visual evidence is available. In the following list, for instance, each item presents an incomplete visual array, yet any adult reader can readily identify it.

1. *Fragmented print*
    hook (book)   *page* (page)   *Christmas* (Christmas)

    William (William)   *John* (John)   *summer* (summer)

2. *Missing letters*
    ol d y   E ster   w a ev r

3. *Missing words*
    When I   John at the corner   knew at   that
    was ill.

4. *Missing letters and words*
    I wa wit cons der le d sm y th I ead th let r.

There are three main reasons why any skilled reader can make sense of incomplete visual evidence. Firstly, he has learned to perceive distinctive features efficiently. Secondly, he can exploit the redundancy (the rich abundance of clues) in the symbols of print and also in the grammar of English. Thirdly, he can reflect on what he is reading and relate it to his prior knowledge of English, the knowledge of the language he brings to any act of linguistic communication. As we shall see, these three types of skill underlie all efficient reading.

In some way we do not as yet understand, each person carries in his brain a number of feature lists; there are feature lists for letters, for words and for segments of text that are longer than words. To identify a grapheme you must locate it in a category of some kind, the category being the 'name' of the letter or word. The distinctive features possessed by a particular grapheme form a unique combination which allows you to allocate it to its category. When you see the grapheme *b* you assign the symbol to the category 'b'; you will assign the graphemes b, *b* to the same category because their features are compatible with the distinctive features for that category, even though there are slight typescript differences.

Occasionally you may come across a grapheme that is so unusual that you find it difficult to assign it to any category. When such a grapheme is a letter you will decide that it is not English; if it occurs in a word, you may decide that the printer has made a mistake. If the unknown grapheme is a whole word and you have no category in which to locate it this means that you don't know that word. In such cases, it may be possible to identify the grapheme by deduction – by 'guessing' its meaning from the context.

When you see the grapheme *bit* you assign it to the category 'bit' because you have perceived various distinctive features that 'signal' that category. If the evidence you have to work on is only one grapheme (as is the case here in this paragraph) you can only assign it to the broad category which comprises that one word in all its meanings. Obviously, with more evidence, you could assign it to a sub-category and give it a more specialized meaning.

There are two main methods of identifying the grapheme *bit*. You could identify the letter *b*, then the letter *i*, then the letter *t*, attach a sound-symbol to each, string them together and sound out the word *bit*; then you could assign the sound 'bit' to a meaning category. Alternatively (and most probably) you can identify the whole grapheme at once, without sounding it out, locating it immediately in a meaning category. This latter method is how skilled readers identify words. The former, rather lengthy, process is how beginner readers identify words. The beginner uses *mediated* identification. The skilled reader uses *immediate* identification. This does not mean *instant* identification, but rather *not mediated*, that is, identifying the meaning of a grapheme without going through the process of linking phonemes and categorizing the sounded-out unit.

Children are taught to identify words by means of mediation. All reading teaching methods involve mediated identification, in that the child has to reach the meaning of graphemes by means of in-termediate procedures. The 'phonics approach' requires the child to learn the sounds of letters and syllables – the teacher trains him to use the mediating actions of identifying letter-sounds and stringing them together to form word-sounds. The 'look-and-say' approach requires the child to identify whole-word graphemes – by means of 'flash-cards' and 'word boxes' the teacher introduces him to a basic vocabulary which will appear in his basal reader.

Most teachers use a combination of phonics and look-and-say and a number of reading schemes have been devised to make the procedures more systematic and easier for the child to learn. To render the sound-symbol correspondence more exact, an Initial Training Alphabet of forty-four characters has been invented, but the difficulty of converting to 'traditional orthography' after the basal stage has made this unpopular. Colour codes have been used to aid phonics training, but again this technique has largely been discarded because it costs more in effort than it gains in method. Other schemes have been devised with a view to capturing the interest of the child and so increasing his motivation to learn. The 'sentence method' uses whole sentences from the beginning so that the child may be interested in the material and get early training in making use of the context. The 'language experience' method makes ample use of talk and uses the transcribed language that emerges as the reading matter to be learned. The 'individualized' approach uses combinations of these various methods in a one-to-one situation.

The process of reading is extremely complex: a complete analysis of the skills identified would reveal some 200 factors. The conventional battery of reading skills includes vocabulary skills, comprehension skills and rate skills, and each of these sets can be subdivided into basic skills, which themselves can be subdivided into subsidiary and intermediate skills. This kind of generalization represents a sort of tradition that has grown up during the twentieth century, when many hundreds of books have been written encapsulating the results of thousands of research projects on reading. Reading has, indeed, become something of an obsession among educationists. During the last fifty years there has been a restless search after better teaching methods; there have been many fashions, many new gimmicks. Every now and then new methods have burst onto the scene to be hailed as a breakthrough only to be superseded by some new 'new approach'. The truth is that there is no correct approach, no perfect methodology. Children have learned to read successfully for many centuries, despite wretchedly crude teaching and hostile circumstances. Given the time, the contact with text, the motivation to learn and the attention of a teacher, any normal child will eventually acquire a degree of reading skill.

Many children, however, fail to learn to read *efficiently*. This is because there are different levels of proficiency, each one harder to master than another as we mount the gradient from beginner reading to mature, literate, reflective reading. It is the teacher's task to know the nature of the proficiency which is required for a given stage of maturity and to devise the most suitable kind of experience for accommodating the appropriate skills. The teacher of basal reading has goals and techniques which are very different from those required of the teacher concerned with the higher-order reading tasks of the secondary school. At each stage, the learner is confronted with problems that have to be solved before he can tackle the business of more complex reading.

The beginner reader's first objective is to be able to make immediate identifications of words. He begins by recognizing letters and clusters of letters and learning to identify by reading some linguistic forms he can identify by hearing. The reading process, even at this stage, is more than merely linking graphemes to sounds. Sounding out a word rarely helps you to identify its meaning. (This is a common misconception among teachers.) Sounding out a word merely changes the in-put channel, translating graphic substance into accoustic substance. Unless you can interpret the sound – locate it in some meaning category – you cannot be said to *know* the word. Any reader, for example, could sound out the word *sluptinto*, but that will not tell you its meaning.* It does happen, of course, that a child will 'decode' a grapheme (*table*, for instance) and then, having *heard* the word, will realize what it means. This happens with words children already know through speech acts. But, with the mature reader, this is a rare event: it is only very infrequently that adults know the meaning of a word when they *hear it* without *seeing it*. In other words, reading involves knowing the language *and* its meanings.

It has been suggested that there are three stages in the development of reading skills. The first is the beginner stage, when the pupil requires various mediating procedures, including reading aloud, in order to obtain meaning. The second stage is when the learner needs to 'listen in' to the text while reading orally but without actually sounding out – a kind of sub-vocal reading for the purpose of reconstituting the text for his own benefit. The third stage is when the student can read silently, obtaining meaning directly from text.[34] But whether or not an aural stage is necessary in reading development, oral reading is the only practicable way in which the teacher can monitor the reading process as the child is operating. It is consequently the only way we can provide the beginner with *feedback* to assist his learning. But it is better to think of oral reading as a means to an end and not an end in itself. The proper objective of all reading training is the ability to read silently and reflectively – what may be called *literate reading*.

Literate reading is the extracting of information from a text

---

* Nobody knows the meaning of *sluptinto*, which is a word I have invented.

without the mediating operations of phonic analysis or vocalization. Literate reading is very different from the kind of letter-by-letter serial scan that the beginner reader employs. If a skilled adult reader were to proceed from letter to letter, sounding them out the way a beginner does, he could not possibly read at a pace faster than, say, 30 to 40 words per minute. In fact, a good literate reader can average at least 300 words per minute. Obviously literate reading proceeds in a very different manner. Of course, the beginner does not remain for long at the stage of sounding out letters; soon he will learn to discriminate the distinctive features of whole words. If he knows these words his mind can leap straight from the visual array to the meaning. Then he will enter a phase in which he proceeds serially from word to word, seeing each word separately. Even a skilled reader will read slowly in this way when tackling a difficult text – for example, when construing Latin or studying a densely technical passage of unfamiliar prose. What happens is that during a fixation (that is the moment at which the eyes fix on a piece of text and take in the visual evidence) the slow reader will linger longer, taking in more visual information about each word than the fast reader needs.

This lack of speed, which seriously handicaps the beginner, is not the result of slow eye movements, as so many people used to think. When scientific research on reading began, late in the nineteenth century, much was made of the way the eye jerked along the line of print as a person read. This eye-jerk, or *saccade*, was thought to be a regulated movement which could be speeded up with training. In fact it is not during a saccade that reading occurs but during a fixation, when the brain is processing the visual information picked up by the eye. There is little difference between the rate of fixations made by slow and fast readers. The skilled reader's eye makes many saccadic movements all over the page, backward as well as forward, but what makes him a skilled reader is not fast fixating but the amount of information he can process during a fixation.

'Rapid Reading' courses which are commercially advertised usually claim to teach the client to read 'three to ten times faster'. When speed reading courses originated in the 1920s and 1930s, much reliance was placed on mechanical methods of training the eyes, but nowadays few commercial courses do more than exhort the client to read faster.[35] Rapid reading courses may well effect improvements in the reading proficiency of strongly motivated students, but not because there is any magic way of speeding up eye-movements. Progress will be made because the client will learn certain reading strategies and because during a course in reading he will probably practise reading intensively in ways he has never experienced before.

Reading faster, then, is not a matter of speeding up the rate of fixations. It is a matter of taking in more information per fixation. It is a question of speeding up the process of identification, and then increasing the chunks of information taken in. The learner quickens his identifying by means of sheer practice in reading – not going over the same text again and again but seeing the same distinctive features and decoding them successfully. It is of crucial importance that the pupil should get as much feedback as possible during this process. For the beginner, the easiest way of giving feedback is by telling him any word or syllable he may not be sure about. As he reads aloud, read with him and instantly provide any information he hesitates over. But feedback need not be verbal – just 'M-hm' may be sufficient confirmation of correct identification. At this stage, practice in feature analysis is essential, so reading aloud with ample feedback needs to be a frequent occurrence. That your skill in feature analysis grows with practice can be seen when you take up crossword puzzles – the more you tackle solving anagrams the more quickly you can do it.

Since efficient reading requires more than a word-by-word scan, the beginner must be encouraged to 'get on with' his reading, even at the expense of accuracy in identifying individual words. A child may make partial identifications more often than the teacher realizes. Unfortunately, the beginner may be unable to signal uncertainty except by saying nothing, so the teacher cannot provide help. In practice reading, it pays to have a natural friendly relationship so that the pupil can verbalize his hesitancy or ignorance. Sometimes a child may venture a bit of a word – for instance, the segment *bro* in *brother* – and stick there; in such a case the teacher should supply the whole word at once and let the pupil go on and get the gist of the message. Parents are sometimes convinced that their child is better at reading at home than the teacher says he is. This may well be because the child is more relaxed at home, readier to offer partial identifications and guesses, altogether more venturesome in his reading. Lack of speed caused by lack of confidence is one of the beginner's major weaknesses.

Another, and in the long run much more important, weakness in the young beginner is his general lack of linguistic knowledge. In reading, the information supplied by the brain is much greater than the information provided by the eye. Skilled reading is much more than the mere ability to translate graphemes into speech. The graphemic substance has to be related to the semantic world. Success in reading depends at least partly on competence in the other linguistic skills and also on general cognitive abilities. Thus reading practice must occur within a rich environment of language experience: such activities as conversation, story-telling, word-games and role-playing enlarge the linguistic store that good reading draws upon. With older pupils the enrichment of general language experience is also a concomitant of progress in reading. For this reason anything that stimulates and extends language-using techniques – exploring themes, talking out problems, discussing stories and so on – will be beneficial to reading competence. Illiterate adults often learn to read very quickly, because they take to the reading act a larger store of general linguistic experience.

As we have seen, the literate reader does not sound out the text but proceeds directly from the visual array to the meaning. Because the efficient, mature reader seems to 'see through' the text into its meaning, reading has been defined as 'externally guided thinking' or 'thought-getting'.[36] One of the major characteristics of language which the good reader exploits is its redundancy. In every sequence of language, whether spoken or written, there is an abundance of clues as to what it means. Words contain more redundant information than do single letters. This redundancy reduces the amount of featural information that needs to be discriminated in any letter position to less than the amount needed for identifying the letter in isolation. What happens is that each letter 'borrows' identity from its relationship with all the other letters. Thus graphic redundancy enables one to identify a word without consciously perceiving every letter.

Another aid to efficient reading is sequential redundancy: that is, the evidence that enables you to predict the complete form before you come to the end. This happens with words (as we have seen, p. 49) and also with phrases and sentences. So powerful is the role of redundancy that the literate reader will be at a disadvantage without it whereas the beginner is not. An experiment which demonstrates this took the form of giving pupils two versions of the same short story. In one version (the U text) the spaces between words were left unfilled; in the other version (the F text) the spaces were filled up with meaningless symbols. The beginner readers, who were still at the stage of looking from letter to letter, were not affected much by the filled-in spaces. But the literate readers, who were used to exploiting orthographic and syntactic redundancies and who needed the blank spaces as cues about where to look, showed a marked decrease in the efficiency of their reading.[37]

The literate reader 'samples' a text, reconstructing the writer's meaning by piecing together the clues he picks up from various features – the grammar, the spelling patterns, the graphic configurations, the collocations* and so on. Thus he can vary his speed

* Collocations are words that a lexical item commonly keeps company with: milk, for example, collocates with *honey, water* etc. but also with *bottle, glass* etc.

of reading by varying the amount of information he uses for his guessing. An 'easy', highly readable text such as a light novel can be read very quickly, at a rate of up to 1000 words per minute. The sampling process, however, is not a case of identifying fewer words. It is a matter of neglecting or passing over information at the featural level, exploiting the various kinds of redundancy carried by the language. The skilled reader uses featural information thinly spread. Thus he is often incapable of remembering the *actual words* of a text; what remains in his memory store is the *meaning*. This has been demonstrated by an experiment with French–English bilinguals. They were given passages such as *His horse, followed de deux bassets, faisait la terre resonner under its even tread* and seemed just as able to understand the passages as unilingual ones.[38] Again, a child seeing a poster saying *Premier Smith Speaks* will just as readily report it as saying *The Prime Minister Talks*. Indeed, a skilled reader will often *add* meaning to a passage, giving it perhaps more significance than it originally contained. This happens frequently in discussing poems.

The young literate reader has to become a mature literate reader. This means that he learns, with experience, to become a more efficient strategist in dealing with a text. His reading skills improve as his knowledge increases – his knowledge of the world, of the ways of writers, of the subject dealt with in each book. Besides extracting the meaning from a text, he reflects upon its message, its form, and its style. He can make prior decisions as to his reading strategies before he tackles a text. The seventeenth-century philosopher, Francis Bacon, was aware that different texts need to be treated in different ways. In his essay, 'Of Studies', he says: 'Some books are to be tasted, others have to be swallowed, and some few to be chewed and digested: that is, some books are to be read only in parts; others to be read, but not curiously; and some few to be read wholly, and with diligence and attention.' The strategic decisions to be made before (and also during) an act of reading have to do with the speed at which the text is to be dealt with, the degree of attention the text will get, the amount of sampling the text will bear without becoming hard to read, and so on.

When meeting a text the mature reader has to be conscious of the text as an artefact and aware of the writer as the maker of it. He knows that there are features of the text which will exhibit the writer's intentions and rhetorical strategies. Every piece of writing contains a liberal amount of evidence to suggest these strategies. Some writers, for example Fielding, Sterne, Thackeray, are explicit about them – 'The next chapter, dear reader, need not delay the impatient . . .' Every skilled reader must learn the so-called 'higher skills' such as sampling, skimming, scanning, reviewing and so on. *Sampling* is reading selected portions. *Skimming* is looking over a text to get an impression of what it deals with. *Scanning* is reading through a text in order to seek and find specific information. *Reviewing* is flipping back to relocate a piece of information.

Children must learn the higher-order skills through experience in the classroom. Many children seem to remain unaware that adults treat books in a variety of ways – they assume that adults read through every book from beginning to end, since this is the treatment they are expected to give a textbook in class. The more children are encouraged to treat books in different ways the better. Before a book is even taken up the pupil should be encouraged to discuss strategies: 'Where shall I sit?' – 'What is it about?' – 'How long will it take?' – and so on. He needs to know that texts can be read in different places, positions and postures for different reasons and at different speeds. Children need to be encouraged, too, to perceive texts as other people's writing efforts: some children think that everything in print is in some measure sacred, and classroom criticism should be encouraged and taught. There is only one way to develop efficiency in reading, namely by reading. Availability is the most important single condition necessary – a rich reading environment, with ample choice, plentiful opportunity, interested people with whom to talk about texts, informed people to suggest books and give encouragement to read them.

Intensive or reflective reading is perhaps the most potent mode of learning available to anyone. In this process the reader has entered into a kind of dialogue with the writer; he is in communion with the author's mind, sometimes, to a certain extent, paying little attention to his language, sometimes studying the language critically as part of a continuous process of judgement-making. Continuously, as he reads, he is getting a multiplicity of hints from the text as to what he should be thinking, how he should be reading and how he should be responding to the author's thinking. A good writer is, by definition, sensitive to this role in his reader and he works hard, through his own techniques and guesswork, to collaborate with the reader he postulates for himself. The comprehension of a passage involves a number of skills: the ability to identify a key sentence; the ability to perceive logical relationships; the ability to perceive the meanings of ambiguities; the ability to infer a conclusion from an indirect assertion. These are essentially cognitive skills – you need them to understand what you hear as well as what you read. Students can be helped to develop them in the course of reading lessons, when the teacher can give them guidance on strategies and encourage them to work hard at reading. But these skills cannot be taught in any real sense: there are no formulae or general rules that lead to greater efficiency. There are really only two ways of helping pupils to develop efficiency in mature, literate reading. One is the 'close reading lesson'; the other is vocabulary building activities.

The 'close reading lesson' is a valuable activity for any age-group of learners.[39] Four conditions are necessary to make it productive: the pupils in the group should be fairly homogeneous in their intellectual capacity, cultural grounding and personal tastes; the language should not be too complex or obscure for them to accommodate; the subject-matter should be interesting; above all, the teacher should be capable of leading the group effectively in the analysis and discussion of the text. The lesson consists simply of questioning and answering in order to 'milk' the text of its meanings and of the evidence which yields the meanings. The aim of the lesson is a full (or fuller) understanding of the text and an appreciation of how the text comes to convey that understanding. Rhetorical analysis of style, paragraph and sentence structures and other textual features must be accompanied by logical analysis of the author's argument or artistic message. Teachers may differ as to the emphasis they place on linguistic as distinct from intellectual study. Either will help the student, but the teacher who can exploit the close reading lesson as a study of language as well as of thought will be the more effective reading teacher.

This is the best way a parent can help an older child (one who can easily decode) to become more competent at the reading process. Seek and sieze upon some enthusiasm which can be fulfilled by reading. Share the enthusiasm if possible and share the reading. Talk together about the subject, the author (his mistakes and follies if they are evident), the words, the meanings of sentences. Cooperate in teasing out difficult or obscure meanings. Collaborate in finding more varied and better written texts. Talk about books, articles, manuals that convey (well or badly) the information you need.

These activities help to increase the 'wordpower' which underlies efficient reading. Reading, like listening, talking and writing, draws upon the general linguistic store which we call communicative competence. The more English you know, the better you perform all the acts of communication and you build up your mastery of English by using it in ever-increasing variety. Thus efficient reading both results from and contributes to the other processes of conveying and receiving meaning. As a means of learning and as a means of communication, 'English' is a seamless robe.

Writing

Writing is the least studied of all forms of communication. Considering the thousands of studies extant on reading, it is surprising that the basic skill of communicating on paper should have been so little researched. What scholarship does exist on writing is mainly concerned with the classification of composed text. Texts produced by mature, skilled authors have, of course, been subjected to intense and sophisticated scrutiny in the form of literary criticism. Texts produced by children in school have been studied with a view to giving teachers descriptive and evaluative guidance, allowing them to compare different compositions and to assess pupils' efforts in subjective as well as normative terms, judging them against various standards.[40] But we do not as yet have a well-developed psychology of writing, nor anything like a rationale for the writing process such as we have for the reading process. Significant work is proceeding, however, and it is possible to make some general observations about the processes whereby children and adults transfer their ideas, experience and feelings into written form.

Many people may believe that writing does not deserve the same attention that is given to other language skills.[41] It is said, with some justice, that speech so predominates in everyday communication that the importance of writing is comparatively slight. It is true that writing is the least common language activity in our society. After they have left school most people cease having to write much: an occasional letter or postcard, notes to the milkman, grocery lists and so on. The amount of writing done by an individual might, in fact, be a fairly good marker of social status. Certainly, if we knew more about the social ecology of writing – when and where and by whom it is done – we would gain interesting insights into the nature of our society.

But writing is still a most important social instrument. It is by far the most common form of long-distance and long-term communication. Our libraries abound with books and it will probably be a long time, if ever, before the present-day proportion of books and tapes is reversed. Taped records are not nearly so readily available as written records, nor are they so easily used. Our educational system rightly puts a high value on writing. It is by far the most important medium for the formal transmission of knowledge, ideas and verbal artefacts and it remains the most effective and practical medium of educational assessment. It is therefore of great importance that we should know more about writing, both as a process and as a product.

One reason why so little attention has been paid to writing until recent years was the prevalent assumption that writing is just 'speech written down'. Teachers assumed, as many still do, that the learning of writing involves only two procedures: firstly, giving the pupils access to handwriting skills; secondly, giving them access to the orthography (the spelling system) of their mother tongue. Given these skills, it was thought, all the other requisites of composition in writing would follow in due course. But writing is not just speech written down. There are distinct and important differences between spoken and written English and for effective learning it must be understood that the writing system of the language has its own rules and conventions.

The raw material of written texts, the graphic substance, includes letters, numbers, punctuation marks and spaces. *Graphology*, the term used by some linguists to parallel *phonology*,[42] includes orthography and all the devices used by the language for carrying grammatical, lexical and rhetorical messages on the writing surface. In broad outlines, of course, the grammar of written English closely resembles that of spoken English and they may be thought of as being basically the same. But there are differences. One important dissimilarity is that speech possesses intonational signals which writing does not carry. For this reason certain written English constructions are ambiguous when spoken: for example, *Parking is restricted to customers only after 9 a.m.*[43] Another important difference is that there are many grammatical forms used in written English which are not used in spoken English – or if they are the speaker would be said to 'talk like a book'. An example of the purely written-English grammatical form is the non-restrictive relative clause. We may *write* a sentence like *The man, who was sick, was carried out* but we would not *say* it. In spoken English we rarely, if ever, make any effort to distinguish between the non-restrictive and restrictive relative clauses; commonly we make little use of *who, which* or *that* for this purpose. In speech we can use redundancy which, in writing, would be avoided: for instance we might say, *The man he was sick you see so they carried him out.*

Another example of difference between spoken and written English is the signalling of common plural nouns. In written English, there are only two signals: -*s* and -*es*. In spoken English, there are three signals: -*s*, -*z*, and -*iz*. Thus we have *cats, dogs* and *houses*. There are also distinctly different ways of signalling the structure of utterances. Spoken English has a complex system of signals to show stress and intonation. Written English has only a few devices such as the question mark, italics, the exclamation point, and these give so little guidance that, when writing, we tend to avoid having to rely upon them. Written English has signals of its own, such as commas, brackets, and quotation marks, which have no parallel in the spoken form. When we read a piece of written English aloud, we 'translate' from one form into another, and we have to put our own interpretation on many of the written English forms. Another important contrast is the different scale of values placed upon certain deviant forms by many people: for instance many people, including many teachers, will not accept 'It was him' in writing, while not even seeing it as deviant in speech.

The most important difference between speech and writing is that writing requires orthographic rules. The need for an agreed orthography is even more of a nuisance than the need for an agreed pronunciation system and we are less tolerant of deviant spellings than we are of deviant pronunciations. You can say *tomato* and I can say *tomayto* and we shall think none the less of one another, but if I spell it with three *t*'s you will ascribe this to my ignorance.*

Orthography is a wholly man-made invention and the rules and techniques have to be learned. Because of this children seldom begin writing until they begin school. It is true that most children know a good deal about writing long before they are five. They know that it consists of marks on paper and that it can be made with pencils, pens, chalk and so on. They know that writing 'says' things to grown-ups; they know that it has to be read. Many will have done some 'pretend writing' in nursery class or at home; some will even have produced some 'invented spelling' – approximations characteristic of children's first efforts. But it is only when they are being taught directly that most children begin to experience the activity of writing. As taught in the old-fashioned schoolroom it was a daunting experience – long, weary sessions of handwriting the letters of the alphabet between the printed lines of a copybook. Nowadays, in the modern classroom, it starts as play and is often associated (as in the 'Breakthrough to Literacy' scheme[44]) with reading and talk. Since it is necessary for the child to be strongly motivated to develop writing skills, modern teachers generate the practical efforts of writing in interesting contexts. Vocabulary building activities are important for efficient reading; they are doubly important for competent writing. Hence the best stimuli to writing are the desire to write and having something to say in writing.

---

* The social importance of correct spelling was dramatically illustrated in 1978 in the case of a typist who, at an industrial tribunal, won her claim for compensation for wrongful dismissal. Miss X submitted that she had been sacked for pointing out a spelling error made by her employer. The employer later maintained that press reports of the case caused him undue embarrassment and insisted that the newspapers carry a statement to the effect that Miss X had frequently made spelling errors in the past.

As we have seen, young children acquire, as the main part of their communicative competence, the skills for putting words together in meaningful relationships. These skills are developed for, and by means of, oral communication. Writing requires much more sophisticated skills which are acquired only by learning certain rules. For in speech you can repeat yourself, retract, break off in the middle of a construction and try another one. But in writing this facility is not available; it is, in fact, a highly skilled activity to represent speech in writing. In writing you have to construct each utterance so that it has a certain finiteness of form. You are unable to use illocutionary devices since you are at a distance, both in space and time, from your interlocutor. Even when you have a *real* interlocutor, as when writing a personal letter, you are out of contact. For all these reasons, writing is a taught competency, which relies on knowledge and practice for its development. It is a premeditated act. You have to decide, deliberately, that you are going to write something; and you have then to make all kinds of decisions about what and how and where you are going to write. Unlike reading, which provides an external guide to shape your thinking for you, writing demands and draws upon your own personal resources. Unlike speaking, which is mostly a form of natural human behaviour, writing is highly conscious, planned action.

It is true that certain spoken utterances are first formed fully and consciously in the mind: when we say that someone spoke deliberately we mean that he mentally rehearsed what he said. In writing, the mental rehearsing is a prerequisite of the action. What happens is that a mentally formed utterance is somehow translated into writing by means of a complex chain of neural, physiological and physical actions: how this happens we do not know.

The psychology of writing is still largely undiscovered: the description I have given is probably much too primitive. There are many other features of the process to be taken into account. It would seem, for example, that fluent writing requires consciousness of the flow of language. James Britton calls this a 'speech-like flow'. He describes an experiment in which he and some colleagues tried writing of various kinds without being able to read what they were writing. Both in handwriting and typewriting they found the task difficult. Although there was no great difficulty in writing a letter to a friend, they experienced 'some handicap' in writing a story, and they felt 'considerable frustration' in writing a research report.[45] It would seem that the gap between writing down a 'spurt' of language and then reading what you have written is filled by certain necessary mental activity. You need to monitor your writing continuously so that you are not, in effect, getting rid of the mental utterance but rather transforming it and maintaining control over it. This means that writing is, after all, something like written-down speech. The act of forming shapes on paper is a kind of extra behaviour you impose upon the act of forming the utterance. But it is not a matter of transcribing speech; it is rather a process of writing down utterances which have been mentally shaped *for* writing – something like 'writing down written English'.

Proficiency in writing and proficiency in reading are both manifestations of a general ability to work with language. But there is also a close functional connection between reading and writing skills. The act of writing is the act of committing to paper written-English forms, and the basic skill is therefore that of creating written-English forms. The more familiar you are with written-English forms the easier you will find it to create them. Reading develops one's knowledge of written English. It is well-known that it is easier to write about something soon after you have been reading about it, and that when you do you tend to employ the constructions that appeared in the read text. The syntactical and lexical material of the text remains in the memory and is drawn upon in the process of writing. The skills of literate reading, such as the ability to 'chunk' information and relate it to its context, are mirrored in the skills of writing. It seems to be necessary to be able to think up a 'chunk' of written-English, to write it down quickly, and then to retain it in the memory long enough and accurately enough to be able to link another chunk to it. Reading back over what you have written clearly helps, but the more skilled you become the bigger the chunk you can retain in your memory. The beginner thinks in small chunks – word by word – and has to regress with high frequency to link his next chunk to the last one. As he becomes more skilled he writes more fluently, regressing less frequently, able to review longer sequences at a time.

If we revert momentarily to the theory of language generation (pp. 21–27) we can describe writing as a process of converting deep structures into graphic representations by means of transformational rules. The deeper components, whether syntactic or semantic, form the ideas. This formulation, the fundamental unfinished sentence, is then transformed into the finished *thought* sentence. By means of the rules learned for the purpose of turning thought into writing (the morphographemic component) we produce the written 'chunk'. When speaking deliberately we listen to and 'edit' the flow of language we are emitting. When writing, which is a much slower activity, we can do this editing more efficiently. It may be that the deeper components generate crude approximations to the finished sentences of our finalized composition and that a good deal of editing goes on mentally. The act of encoding an idea in writing may include features that resemble the act of decoding and the practised literate writer may well be able to proceed from the meaning intended to the written message without actually having to internalize a written-English sentence at all. Thus it may be sensible to say 'How do I know what I mean until I see what I have written?' Much of this speculation, however, remains to be researched.

The most obvious difficulty faced by the child is his inability to write quickly by hand. His inability to form the shapes on paper must, of course, prevent him from transmuting his thoughts into written form. But lack of skill with the reproductive mechanisms can be overcome. Some reading-and-writing schemes such as The Schools Council's 'Breakthrough to Literacy' have devised 'sentence-maker' cards to enable children to record utterances without the need to hand-write. By using tape-recorders, teachers can help train children to compose orally. The constraints imposed by having to dictate might reflect or support the constraints of the somewhat impersonal nature of communicating in writing. The point is that the child is *composing* rather than speaking, and the construction-forming process involved is the basic element of writing. But these contrivances, valuable in themselves, merely postpone the necessity of learning to write. Handwriting must still be learned by anyone who is to be literate. In the future, when we have access to computerized voice-activated writing machines, it may be possible to dispense with handwriting for most purposes. But these machines will not do the composition for the user and it will still be necessary to think out what is to be set down, to encapsulate the message in language and to operate all the higher order skills needed for proficient communication.

Learning to write competently is a process of building up experience of various kinds: experience of using language for communication; experience of conceptualizing written-English forms; experience of reproducing these forms in acceptable sequences, in acceptable orthography, in effective organizational patterns. In order to help develop these forms of experience the teacher must pay attention to the characteristics of different kinds of writing. Like spoken discourse, written English takes on different grammatical, lexical and stylistic characteristics in accordance with the writer's purpose. A telegraphed message, a newspaper article, a literary essay, a note to the milkman, will each carry the features required to fulfil its particular function. Experience of these features is a necessary element of learning to write competently.

Various typologies of writing have been proposed. One valuable scheme of categories is that developed by James Britton and his colleagues in the London Writing Research Unit. This scheme is based in part on the distinction between using language in the role of participant and that of spectator.[46] There are three main categories: *transactional writing, expressive writing* and *poetic writing*. Transactional writing is produced when the writer is in the participant role, and poetic writing emerges when the writer is in the spectator role. Expressive writing is the central term, and Britton suggests that it is 'a kind of matrix' from which differentiated forms of writing will be evolved.[47] This is the most 'natural' or 'personal' form of writing, and it is the base from which children move into the other forms. Expressive writing is nearest the child, most accessible to him, and it is in this form that he can explore his own thoughts and feelings. It is less rule-governed, more spontaneous than the other modes. If we attribute psychological reality to the 'expressive function' in writing, it would be akin to the *personal function* of language in Halliday's categorization (see p. 43).

Transactional writing is the mode used for *doing things:* recording, reporting, arguing, regulating. This is the kind of writing used in the business of living. As expressive writing moves into the transactional mode it will become more explicit, more concerned with accuracy. Transactional writing is used to present information, and it is the kind most used in school: for the making of notes, essays, examination answers, and many other purposes. Poetic writing is writing valued for its own sake, as an end in itself. This kind of writing is artefact, consciously produced (in essays, stories and poems) to be contemplated and enjoyed by a reader.[48]

Useful though this classification may be, it cannot yet be said whether it yields rules for the teaching or assessing of composition techniques. It offers insights into the nature of writing, but it remains to be seen whether there is a genuine relationship between the *kinds of composition* described in the scheme and the ways of composing. There is no evidence to show any kind of psychological reality in these categories. But clearly each kind of writing can be shown to require, for its successful realization, the implementation of certain rules. These rules may be called the rules of rhetoric, which is the theory and practice of verbal composition and which is the subject of a section in my next chapter (see p. 103).

The teaching of writing (that is, of composition) has been much neglected, mainly because of our ignorance of its nature and provenance. Teachers generally assume, erroneously, that a piece of writing is 'thought' written down. But writing should not be equated with thought. Written composition of any kind is thought which has been mediated by the act of writing. The difference is clearly evident when you contrast a pupil's oral treatment of an idea with his treatment of the same idea in a completed piece of writing. A pupil's spoken treatment can often be lucid and potent while the same pupil's written effort may be disorganized, stilted and inaccurate. This is not only because in speech you can freely reiterate and reshape your thinking, but also because the confidence and freedom most of us possess in speaking is much reduced when we come to write. The reductive pressures of writing – having to handwrite or type, having to rehearse mentally what you propose to write, having to find the right words and so on – constitute a barrier to free self-expression. The easy flow on to paper that a skilled writer can demonstrate when he is familiar and confident in his subject soon becomes sluggish when he is dealing with a different subject. Young students find the reductive pressures frustrating, especially when, as nearly always happens, they lack confidence or motivation to write. Good teaching must begin with contriving circumstances within which writing becomes enjoyable or, at the very least, highly desirable. Since it is nearly always more pleasurable to talk about something, a good writing lesson must be an occasion when writing is not a boring substitute for talk but the necessary and only suitable form of communication. And, in teaching writing, we must help the pupil to translate his thought into written English that carries the same amount of logical and expressive force that he can achieve in talk.

There are seven principles of learning enunciated by Skinnerian 'operant learning' theorists, and all of these can be applied to the teaching of writing.[49]

1. *Concentrate on the individual organism*
   Teachers tend to concentrate on the written production, rather than on the pupil. It is as if a piano teacher did nothing but analyze and judge his student's performance of a piece of music. In a real sense most teachers hardly ever *teach* writing at all: they only assess it. It is necessary for the teacher to study *the pupil writing*, not the *pupil's writing*. One-to-one teaching and immediate guidance are essential to effective teaching of writing; sitting with the pupil, the teacher can discuss the pupil's intentions, accept and discuss his oral offering, guide it into writing, reinforce it with suggestions for vocabulary, phrasing, paragraphing, imagery and other features of rhetoric.

2. *Build from the naive behavioural repertory*

This is the pupil's own 'natural' offering – if you like, his expressive utterance. Its great value is that it is the pupil's own response, and the teacher should begin from that. Teachers are prone to judge the *product*, but they should pay attention to the *producer*. They should make sure that his producing is encouraged, that the act of composing is carried forward. They can do this by attending to and rewarding the pupil's approximations – what is nearly right – rather than his errors.

3. *Work with freely emitted behaviour*

The pupil should decide what he wants to write. Let him write what he likes writing. Whether it is expressive or transactional or poetic is irrelevant. If it is voluntarily done it will be good material to work on.

4. *Ensure a high frequency of response*

Pupils should have many opportunities to learn the skills of writing. An essay a month is of no use. A golfer working on his swing takes a bucketful of balls to the practice ground and puts himself in a high-response situation. Giving a pupil an essay to do once a month (or even once a week) is analogous to the golf pro making his pupil do a round of eighteen holes every time he gives a lesson. Writing skills will only develop with frequent lessons in a skilfully controlled environment.

5. *Ensure a low duration of response*

The teacher should require a large number of short writing tasks rather than a few long ones. But they must be *writing tasks*, not one-word answers or slot-fillings for exercises. Devising frequent short writing tasks which are also enjoyable and freely undertaken is certainly not easy, but this is a requirement of good teaching.

6. *Reinforce the desired response immediately*

Marking an exercise days after it was written is of little value. The pupil's skill should be strengthened *as he is writing* and a good feature – a telling phrase, for example, or a well-constructed sentence – should be rewarded with praise *during* the writing lesson. On-the-spot advice is very much more effective than a cold appraisal after the event.

7. *Shape the behaviour through intermediate specification of the response*

A pupil gains little or nothing from a remark in the margin or a pencilled stroke under an error. The golfer must adjust his movement on his *next* swing, not during his next full round of the course. The pianist must correct his fingering at once. Effective teaching of writing should be given while the pupil is at his task, so that he can make immediate use of his teacher's guidance.

All of these 'rules' amount to the simple message that writing should be taught while the pupil is actually at work. That is why skilled modern teachers speak of 'writing clinics' and long for more time, smaller class groups, more opportunities to give each pupil personal attention. Pupils who are lucky enough to get this kind of help – whether at home or at school – cannot fail to become as competent in writing as their general capacity allows. Like reading, writing is a highly complex activity and, like reading, writing is learned best by doing it.

Spelling

In *The Girl's Own Paper* published on 5 October 1889 the following item appears in the 'Answers to Correspondents' column:

> Mary B – We know of no way to improve the spelling, save by looking out each word in the dictionary, and writing doubtful words several times over till you remember them.

Poor Mary B. would not have profited much from that advice and her great-grandchildren will not be much better served. Almost all teachers are in the grip of a fallacy about English spelling which has been held for centuries, namely that the orthography is a crazy, unsystematic mess. This arises from the notion that it is supposed to represent the sounds of English. It is true that English orthography is to some extent a sound-to-spelling system. There are some 46 phonemes in English, but only 26 letters in the alphabet. There are, therefore, phonemes which need combinations of letters to represent them – for example, the sounds represented by *ng* in *sing*, *th* in *thief*, *th* in *those*, *ch* in *chess* and so on.

The orthography successfully allows us to transfer all English sounds to writing. But it also allows us to represent the morphemes, the units of meaning, in our writing. For example, if the orthography were merely a sound-to-spelling system the word *marked* would be spelled *markt*, the word *toes* would be spelled *toze* – or some other means would be required to represent the sound of the word phonetically. But *-ed, -es* are essential bound morphemes to signal *past tense* and *plural* respectively: the spelling system preserves these features. The English spelling system also preserves the root morphemes in compound words. In *electric, electricity, electrician,* for example, there are three different pronunciations for the second *c*, but our spelling system allows us to retain the word *electric*. If the

orthography set out to achieve a direct sound-spelling correspondence, we would need a different grapheme in each case.
Similarly the root *sign* is spelled the same in *signing, signal, signify;* in
create, creation and *creative* the root is preserved, and there are many
instances of this morphemic consistency. Thus our orthography is a
morpheme-to-spelling system as well as a sound-to-spelling system.[50]

Orthographics also deals with spelling-to-sound correspondences
and it is unfortunately true that English does not have a phonemic
alphabet with a one-to-one correspondence between the letters and
sounds; this means that English spelling can be confusing for
children reading aloud and for foreign students of the language. The
sources of confusion are vividly illustrated in this poem:

> *Hints on Pronunciation for Foreigners*
> I take it you already know
> Of tough and bough and cough and dough?
> Others may stumble but not you,
> On hiccough, thorough, laugh and through?
> Well done! And now you wish, perhaps
> To learn of less familiar traps?
>
> Beware of heard, a dreadful word
> That looks like beard and sounds like bird,
> And dead: it's said like bed, not bead—
> For goodness sake don't call it 'deed'!
> Watch out for meat and great and threat
> (They rhyme with suite and straight and debt).
>
> A moth is not a moth in mother
> Nor both in bother, broth in brother,
> And here is not a match for there
> Nor dear and fear for bear and pear,
> And then there's does and rose and lose –
> Just look them up – and goose and choose,
> And cork and work and card and ward,
> And font and front and word and sword,
> And do and go and thwart and cart –
> Come, come, I've hardly made a start!
> A dreadful language? Man alive!
> I'd mastered it when I was five![51]

The fact that most of these words can be shown to result from
demonstrable rules is no consolation to the learner, but such is the
case. In the spelling-to-sound system, for example, the following
rules explain the apparent inconsistencies among the *vowel* + *gh*
words:*

* The symbols within braces represent the sounds occurring in the words
listed, and ∅ means zero.

1. $au \rightarrow \{ae\}$ implies $gh \rightarrow \{f\}$:   *laugh, draught*
2. $au \rightarrow \{ɔ\}$ implies $gh \rightarrow \{\phi\}$:   *caught, naught, naughty,*
     taught, daughter, fraught,
     slaughter.
3. $ou \rightarrow \{ə\}$ implies $gh \rightarrow \{f\}$:   *clough, enough, rough,*
     slough, sough, tough
4. $ou \rightarrow \{o\}$ implies $gh \rightarrow \{\phi\}$:   *borough, dough, furlough,*
     thorough, though
5. $ou \rightarrow \{u\}$ implies $gh \rightarrow \{\phi\}$:   *through*
6. $ou \rightarrow \{au\}$ implies $gh \rightarrow \{\phi\}$:   *bough, slough, sough.*[52]

These rules are not all without exceptions, but the words listed for each rule are *all* the words in English which would normally occur in these contexts.* (Such items as *slough* and *sough* occur in two lists because they can be pronounced in two ways.) *Hiccough* (pronounced *hiccup*) is, of course, an exception. Most 'exceptions' in English can be explained historically. They may be borrowings from foreign languages where the foreign spelling has been retained, or they may be old English spellings altered by scribes to show their foreign origin.

The spelling-to-sound system is of little pedagogical importance. It is true that English orthography exhibits massive redundancy, so that awareness of its rules will be of considerable help to the reader. But as we have seen, reading is a competence best acquired by sheer practice and experience rather than conscious application of rules and the characteristics of spelling which are helpful in reading are attended to along with all the other distinctive features of the visual array. English orthography is, in fact, designed for readers well-acquainted with English. It is also partly ideographic in that the letter clusters are perceived as meaningful wholes. Analyses such as those of Venezky and Scragg are of immense value for our understanding of the nature of English and they have great potential value for the construction of systematic reading schemes. But they are essentially academic in character and their usefulness for ordinary pedagogical purposes is not yet evident.

One obvious benefit bestowed on us by linguistic scholarship of this kind is the assurance it gives us that spelling reformers are, for the most part, wrong. There have been spelling reformers for centuries, from *The Ormulum*† of about 1200 AD to the modern

* It would be easy, of course, to find proper names which do not conform to these rules, or to invent non-instances.

† A book of metrical homilies on the gospels written by someone called Orm, the Ormulum is the most valuable extant source of evidence on the Middle English spelling system.

protagonists of Sir James Pitman's Initial Teaching Alphabet. Venezky writes:

> The literature on spelling reform is imbued with a revivalistic quality; it sees the prevailing orthography as the degenerate product of neglect, denseness, and lack of adaptability. It sees the future of the English speaking people, if this malignancy is allowed to remain, as continued degeneration: children falling prey to the corrupted speech of the lower classes, world trade falling off, and business suffering throughout the land.[53]

Most reformers seek a simplified and regularized writing system by means of enlarging what G. B. Shaw called 'our wretched alphabet'.[54] In the sixteenth century, John Hart proposed a reformed alphabet which he claimed would avoid the 'vices' of 'diminution' (too few letters), 'usurpation by one letter of the powers of another' and 'misplacement of letters' (mismatch of spelling and pronunciation as in *what* as spoken in some dialects). Most of his successors campaigned for phonemic systems, criticizing the *status quo* by citing what Venezky calls 'worn-out examples' such as *debt, doubt, victuals*.[55] The most notorious example of the 'absurdity' of English spelling is *ghoti*, which is said to spell out 'fish' because of *gh* as in *tough*, *o* as in *women*, *ti* as in *station*. This is itself an absurdity, of course, since none of these graphemes could occur in these positions in English. Sir James Pitman's Initial Training Alphabet is not in the main-line tradition of spelling reforms, but rather a regularized system designed to make basal reading easier for children. As an experiment this device proved successful but the ITA has been largely given up because of lack of reading materials and a prevalent uncertainty among teachers as to whether it was worth the cost and trouble.

Large-scale and radical reform of our orthography must be rejected on several grounds. In the first place, the reformers have failed to perceive the strength of our spelling system, especially its ability to preserve a morphemic pattern and its preservation of derivational evidence. For example, the retention of *b* in *doubt* reminds us of its origin in the Latin *dubitare*; *debt* comes from Latin *debitum* and the *b* relates the word to *debit*; *victuals* comes from Latin *victualis*. In the second place, spelling reform on a large scale does not appear to be necessary, since the majority of children learn to cope reasonably well with our orthography both in the decoding process of reading and in the encoding process of writing. In the third place, the alteration of the orthography proposed by nearly all the reformers is to make the alphabet a phonemic one, but the irregularities in our spelling system occur just as much in the morphemic system, so a phonemic alphabet would merely create even greater irregularities. Lastly, a large-scale change in the spelling system would be costly and would render millions of books obsolete. When all that has been said, however, it must be realized that our spelling has been continuously reformed over several centuries and it remains true that English spelling *could* continue to be simplified, to the benefit of all, by introducing a few small changes over a period of, say, twenty years: for example, the doubling of consonants could beneficially be extended to secure more consistency, and the alphabet might be a more potent instrument if a few new letters were added. But in the meantime we must be aware that, as Felicia Lamport has put it, 'fonetik speling still haz implikashunz uv unejukatid absurditi'.[56]

The important pedagogical aspect of spelling is its role in the writing process. It is important, first of all, that a pupil should learn to present in writing the words he means to be read and not to convey something different by mistake: for instance, to 'accept an apology' and not 'except' it; to refer to a 'corps' and not a 'corpse' and so on. It is important, too, that words should be spelled correctly because an excess of misspellings creates 'interference' in the communication by distracting the reader. Finally, for our own self-esteem, we should not invite ridicule or contempt by exhibiting lack of skill in a socially important accomplishment.

It has often been suggested, with good reason, that skill in spelling is 'caught, not taught'. Given some competence in using English for talk and reading, the child will readily learn to write English with reasonable accuracy. If you count the number of words correctly spelled in the composition of any normal ten-year-old, you would realize that he scores many more hits than misses and that most of the misses are near-hits and easily recognizable. If writing is carried on in the classroom alongside (and preferably in association with) reading and talk, pupils will generally succeed in learning the orthographic patterns for the function words they use. The graphemic patterns of lexical words 'known' to a normal fluent reader of ten to twelve years of age must be very numerous, running to tens of thousands. The recognition vocabulary is always much greater than the 'active' usage vocabulary that can be reproduced at will; nonetheless the number of words a normal ten-year-old can summon to his pen runs to many thousands. Of these, only a small proportion will present spelling difficulties.

The good teacher of primary school children will avoid fuss over spelling, knowing that although practice may not make perfect it will make them passably competent. But the ten-a-day rote learning of spelling is not the way. It may not do any harm (and it may even do some good by increasing the pupil's familiarity with orthographic conventions), but spelling is a feature of *written* English and it is time-wasting to dissociate it from activities related to writing English. From the very beginning of his association with the written word the child should be encouraged to attend to spelling. The best approach to spelling is to treat it as another interesting aspect of language: thus the 'behaviour' of English words can be studied during early phonics lessons, at more casual times when teacher and child are 'writing together' and during those lessons in which language is encountered as a by-product of other studies.

The spelling 'rules' which are worth examining in class are of two kinds. Firstly, there are the rules that may be called linguistically inherent: these are orthographic consistencies arising from the nature of the words' make-up, such as the gemination (or doubling) of consonants in compounds like *interrupt* and affix-carrying words like *spinning, trotting, expelled*, etc. Secondly, there are rules that have been invented to aid the writer. These have little or no linguistic reasons for existing, being merely consistencies observed and considered worth noting. These 'rules' are nearly always accompanied by a list of exceptions. There is no evidence that direct learning of either kind of rule has a significant effect on the spelling proficiency of the student, but there are two useful features of this activity: one is that in the actual lesson a considerable amount of interest in words might be aroused, the other is that the rules can form a kind of reference list, like a dictionary, to be consulted when needed. I see no reason why children should not be shown how to compile a personal spelling dictionary and in discussing how the words and rules might be classified much might be learned about the language. But the best reference list is the mental one we all build up through experience, and spelling, like all other aspects of language, is best learned by using English in real activities.

This modern approach to teaching spelling skills may give some people the impression that children nowadays are less proficient than they used to be. But signal detection theory tells us that the more efforts you make at decoding – or encoding – signals the more errors you make: that is, you maximize your successes but increase your failures. In the modern primary classroom the pupils are much more adventurous than in the past. The old-fashioned teacher perceived spelling in a negative, punitive fashion, attending only to mistakes and inhibiting pupils from attempting to write anything of which they were not wholly sure. Now children are encouraged to be more experimental, less inhibited. Of course they will make more spelling errors but this is because they will write more words, and attempt more creative writing.

Among the artificial pedagogical 'rules', perhaps the most useful one is that, with all its irregularities, English orthography does represent the pronunciation of words. Mispronunciation inevitably leads to misspelling: indeed, if you do not know the correct pronunciation for a word then good spelling habits *ought* to lead you to misspell it. Thus some people commit such errors as *pronounciation, undoubtably, libary, stricly, atheletics, mischievious, similiar, umberella.* There are, of course, words which we all (or most of us) commonly 'mispronounce' in the sense that we slur over or omit certain phonemes: this is how some people come to make such errors as *artic, genrally, goverment, labratory, reconize.* Then there are words that can be misspelled because the erroneous pronunciation includes intrusive phonemes: thus *hinderance, lightening, rememberance, sufferage,* and so on. This disjunction between our way of sounding certain words and our way of spelling them should be mentioned in class as the opportunities arise. There are so few of these orthographic traps that it is easy to become vigilant for them.

Another important source of observation in class arises from the 'rule' that English spelling preserves a word's derivation *in preference* to its sound. Thus we have many words which appear to disobey the orthographic principles of English because their origin in a different language remains evident in the spelling: for example *description, divide, marriage, privilege, separate,* and many more.

In this category come those words in which it is sometimes difficult to decide whether the suffix should be *-able* or *-ible.* The 'rule' states that *-ible* should be used when the Latin origin ended with *-ibilis* and *-able* should be used for words of distinctly French or English origin. Thus we have more than fifty such spellings as *accessible, admissible, audible, collapsible, credible, eligible, forcible, plausible, visible,* etc., some of which (for example, *collapsable*) have optional alternatives, and an almost infinite list (because *-able* is a 'live suffix' which can be attached to almost any transitive verb) such as *advisable, admittable, believable,* etc. This rule is not very useful because most of us have no idea of the Latin origins. Reference books such as *Fowler's Modern English Usage* or the more comprehensive dictionaries provide guidance. The important teaching point is that pupils should be aware that there *is* room for uncertainty.

A similar source of possible difficulty lies in the words ending in *–ise* or *-ize.* Most of these originate from Greek words ending *-izare.* For this reason American English prefers the ending *-ize* for the majority of words, even for English words taking verb-forms by analogy, such as *botanize, criticize, legalize, memorize, patronize, sterilize*. A number of British printers follow the French practice of making *-ise* the norm, and many British teachers teach the 'rule' 'when in doubt, use *-ise*'. But it is now a house rule with most of the important British publishers that *-ize* should be preferred, and most Australians will give *-ize* the preference where there is an option. Words borrowed directly from French (and not from French via Latin) tend to be spelled *-ise* in American English and in British English it would be incorrect to spell these words otherwise: the most common of these words are *advertise, advise, enfranchise, compromise, demise, despise, devise, disguise, improvise, merchandise, revise, surmise*. Certain words derived from the French verb *prendre* (with the participle *pris* or *prise*) regularly end in *-ise*: *comprise, enterprise, surprise*. It is interesting that *apprise*, meaning to 'inform', is distinguished by our precise English orthography from *apprize* meaning to 'appraise', the former coming from the French *appris* and the latter from the French *aprisier*.

It is worthwhile to let pupils become aware that the different Englishes have developed some different orthographic characteristics. American English spelling has been influenced by the work of Noah Webster, who must be given an honoured place with Samuel Johnson, Tod and Latham among the great lexicographers of English of the last two centuries. Although Webster's attempts to reform English spelling were fiercely resisted and many of his innovations, such as *wimen* and *tung*, were dropped even in his own later dictionaries, he successfully persuaded Americans to drop the *u* from *-our* endings in such words as *colour, honour, armour*, etc.; he replaced *gaol* with *jail*; and he was largely responsible for arousing among his countrymen an interest in words which has steadily increased over the years. The movement toward simplification in American English spelling has resulted in many variant forms. The *ae* and *oe* in words derived from Latin or Greek (*encyclopaedia, anaemia, anaesthetic, faeces, foetus*, etc.) have been replaced by *e* in American English; Australian English still prefers the British spellings but allows the American options; and British English is fast adopting this practice, as in *ecology, ecumenical, etiology* and other words which were formerly spelled with *ae*. British and Australian English have so far resisted Websterian simplification of such words as *centre, metre, fibre, sombre, spectre*, though the new *Heinemann Australian Dictionary* is careful to show the American alternatives. Other American simplifications such as replacing all *-ce, -se* endings with a uniform *-se* (as in *defense, offense, pretense*) and replacing medial *ou* with *o* (as in *mold, smolder, molt*) have not been adopted elsewhere. But the American preference for *-ction* in place of *-xion* has won ground in Britain and Australia: this is an example of the English-speaker's preference for showing morphemic consistency (as in *connection, deflection, inflection*) as against etymological purity, since these words derive from Latin nouns ending in *-xio*. Another American reform which is gaining acceptance in Britain and other English-speaking countries is the dropping of the medial *e* in such words as *judgement, fledgeling, abridgement*, though the desire to preserve morphemic patterns makes many people averse to this trend.

Of course, intercultural variants in spelling are not mistakes, though it would be a mistake to be inconsistent in one's use of any convention: whichever set of conventions you favour, you must adhere to it. Spelling errors are almost always caused by the writer's ignorance of the accepted convention. English abounds in homophones, for example, and it is necessary to know which spelling is appropriate in a given context. Words which are commonly confused are *affect* and *effect*; *allusion* and *illusion*; *canvas* and *canvass*; *capital* and *capitol*; *coarse* and *course*; *compliment* and *complement*; *council* and *counsel*; *holy* and *wholly*; *loath* and *loathe*; *plain* and *plane*; *precede* and *proceed*; *principal* and *principle*; *stationary* and *stationery*. Grammatical items can similarly be confused: *it's* and *its*; *of* and *off*; *their*, *there* and *they're*; *therefor* and *therefore*; *threw* and *through*; *to, too* and *two*; *whose* and *who's*; *your* and *you're*. With some of these latter terms an elementary knowledge of the grammar should suffice to indicate which item is required. With many of the lexical items there is nothing for it but to learn the correct application. Here is where the advice given to Mary B. might help, but it would be better if the words were committed to memory by embedding them in constructions – such as 'Is the holy Bible wholly true?' Sometimes a mnemonic will aid the memory, such as 'He's my princi<u>pal pal</u>' or 'allusion is a literary term' or 'there's <u>a rat</u> in se<u>parat</u>e'. The so-called 'spelling rules' which follow are worth learning by adults or older pupils for whom spelling offers difficulty. They are best remembered through a few examples. The exceptions are usually self-evidently different forms.

The e Rules

When a suffix begins with a vowel, drop the *e*.
When a suffix begins with a consonant, retain the *e*.
Examples:

bride	+ -*al*	= *bridal*		*entire*	+ -*ly*	= *entirely*
fame	+ -*ous*	= *famous*		*grace*	+ -*ful*	= *graceful*

move	+ *-able*	= *movable*		*rude*	+*-ness*	= *rudeness*
prime	+ *-ary*	= *primary*		*state*	+ *-ment*	= *statement*
precede	+ *-ence*	= *precedence*				

Exceptions: due, duly; awe, awful (because we also have *aweful*); *hoe, hoeing; notice, noticeable; courage, courageous* (and so on with all words where the *e* is retained to preserve the 'soft' sound of *c* or *g*).

The Gemination Rules

If a suffix begins with a vowel, double the final single consonant

– for monosyllables
– for stressed syllables
– if the consonant follows a single vowel.

Examples:

wag	*wagging*		*abhor*	*abhorring*
pat	*patting*		*admit*	*admittance*
spin	*spinning*		*remit*	*remitted*
			repel	*repelled*
			regret	*regrettable*

But:

infer – inference, prefer – preference, and *refer – reference* etc. (because the stress is shifted to the first syllable).

And:

profit –profiting, revel – reveler, reveling, etc. (because the stress does not lie on the last syllable).

And:

need – needed, tread – treading (because the consonant does not follow a single vowel).

The e-i Rule

When the sound is *e* write *ie* except after *c*.
When the sound is not *e* write *ei*.

Examples:

ee sound	*after c*	*ay sound*
relieve	conceive	eight
priest	deceive	rein

chief	receipt	veil
siege	ceiling	sleigh
field	perceive	weigh
grieve		reign

Exceptions: either, neither, financier, seize, species, weird.

The y Rule

Change final *y* to *i* except when the suffix is *-ing*.

Examples:

defy – *defiance* – *defying*
happy – *happiness*
mercy – *merciful*
modify – *modified* – *modifying*

These 'rules' have 'just growed' like Topsy – they are neither linguistically inherent nor arbitrary – but in many cases they grow out of the need to represent a vast number of speech-sounds by means of a very much smaller number of available graphemes. The 'rules' presented in dictionaries are only as reliable as the lexicographers' scholarship allows. The English-speaking peoples do not have prestigious national bodies, such as the French Academy, to exercise controls on spelling. Instead, English speakers have invested their faith in certain pundits, like Samuel Johnson, Noah Webster, F. G. and H. W. Fowler, whose works have been widely used for reference. The British Broadcasting Company grew into a kind of unofficial arbiter of pronunciations and coinages during the 1920s and 1930s. Some famous writers and scholars, such as G. B. Shaw, Arthur Lloyd James and Robert Bridges were selected to form an Advisory Committee in 1926. Since their preoccupation was wholly with the spoken tongue, they had nothing to say about spelling, but indirectly their influence was strong. This Committee decided, for example, that *charabanc* should be pronounced as in French, then decided it should be anglicized, then changed their mind again. Their major influence on spelling was that they emphasized – albeit unwittingly – that the English language is not amenable to control by select arbitrators.

Punctuation

Proficient writing requires efficient punctuation, which is simply a set of conventions designed to reinforce the semantic structure of a piece of written communication. The placing of punctuation points is an essential part of the art of writing and it should be learned along with the other conventions. Pupils should realize as early as possible that punctuating is a useful way of helping to indicate meaning, mood and intention. The pupil should be encouraged to use the punctuation markers in the same manner in which he is taught to use capitalization – along with appropriate constructions. Just as he learns to write his own name or *London* or *New York* with appropriate capitals, so he should learn to accompany an exclamation or question with the appropriate point. At an early stage, too, the pupil should realize that punctuation is the only way we have in writing of indicating stress and intonation. They naturally acquire a sense of the sentence and its parts in speech, though they may not be conscious of it. It is essential that they should learn to represent this sentence structure by means of punctuation.

Originally writers of English did not, apparently, find it necessary to divide words by spaces in their manuscripts; and it was well into the seventeenth century before most people began to employ punctuation marks at all. In the sixteenth century Aldus Manutius introduced a regular system of pointing, the signs being derived mainly from the dots used by Greek grammarians. These have often changed their function: for example, the Greeks' interrogative mark is now our semi-colon. Although punctuation marks were used in Sumerian, Hittite, Egyptian and Chinese writing systems, it was only with the development of printing for mass readership that it became common in modern times. Even today, however, punctuation is widely considered to be merely an additional embellishment of written composition rather than an essential feature. Many adults show the paucity of their early training by writing down a sequence of sentences and then 'going back over it' to 'put in' the punctuation.

The Comma

The most important point is the comma, because it signals essential junctures in sentences. The sentence *I spent a week looking after the boys who were sick with fever* has one meaning as it stands here: 'Some of the boys were sick and I spent a week looking after them'. The *who* clause here is a restrictive relative clause; it implies that there were other boys, and it means the same as an adjectival phrase or a simple noun might mean: *I spent a week looking after the feverish boys* or *I spent a week looking after the boys with fever*. With the insertion of a comma to set off the relative clause to make it non-restrictive, the meaning of the sentence is quite different. *I spent a week looking after the boys, who were sick with fever* now means *I spent a week looking after the boys. Incidentally, they were sick with fever.* Here there is no implication that there were other boys.

The comma also sets off non-restrictive phrases: for example, *The children, their eyes shining, ran to meet their friends.* It also sets off appositive phrases: for example, *Johnny, the new cook, met us at the door.*

The comma has three other major functions in the sentence:

1. *It separates clauses joined by* and, but, or, nor, for.

   Examples:
   He asked for food, and I gave him some bread.
   He asked for food, but she refused to give him any.
   He asked for a meal, or at least a little bread.
   He would give her nothing, nor would he encourage her to ask.
   He asked for some bread, for he was weak with hunger.

2. *It sets off introductory clauses and phrases.*

   Examples:

   While the girls set a fire going beside the stream, their parents looked for driftwood along the shore.
   Their ages being almost exactly the same, they were always chosen to play the parts of the twins.

3. *It separates items in a series.*

   Examples:

   Cows, horses, pigs and dogs crowded the pathway.
   They wandered along the path, across the field, up the hill, into the wood.
   He reported that the messengers had arrived, that their story was grim, and that the captain had arranged an assembly for that evening.

The Full Stop

The full stop, or period, marks the logical end of a sentence. Knowing where to place the period depends on knowing what a sentence is, and *that* is a major difficulty for the incompletely trained writer. Despite its unpopularity with modern grammarians, the old definition of a sentence as 'a group of words expressing a complete thought' is still useful. This definition is, certainly, a circular one – a 'complete thought' is a sentence! – but mostly one can recognize the completeness of an utterance when one says it. It is only in formal standard prose that the sentence becomes difficult to perceive, and this is because writing of that complexity tends to embed one utterance within another.

The Question Mark

The question mark should be used only where it is necessary to mark off a genuine question. But it can be used for stylistic purposes to some effect.

Examples:

Who wrote the book? (Direct question)
He asked who wrote the book. (Indirect question)
He asked, 'Who wrote the book?'
Did he tell the story, write the book, sell it?
Did he tell the story? write the book? sell it?

The Exclamation Point

The exclamation point is used sparingly in modern writing. To spatter your page with exclamation points is a sign of immaturity. It is used effectively to mark interjections; also, it can be used to give an exclamatory effect to a sentence.

Examples:

No! I can't believe it!
Give me liberty, or give me death!

The Semi-colon

The semi-colon should be used to mark off parts of a sentence that are equal in grammatical status. It can be used to join together in one sentence utterances that could optionally be separated into sentences. It can also be used to separate phrases which occur as a list in a sentence.

Examples:

I came; I saw; I conquered.
He was a man of immense charm; but his charm was shown only to those he trusted.
The delegation arrives today; in fact, it should be here now.
The book offers many delights to the careful reader, couched as it is in a highly entertaining style; gives promise of even greater amuse-

ment in the second volume; and serves to whet the appetite for what may be a whole series of studies in the subject.

The Colon

The colon is a useful mark, normally used after an introductory statement to direct attention to what follows. It differs from the semi-colon in function, and they cannot be used interchangeably. The colon is a signal, the semi-colon is a separator.

Examples:

Her hobby is obvious: talking.
We have three kinds of cloth: silk, wool and nylon.
There is only one possible explanation: the train was late.
His intentions were plainly stated: to seek election; if elected, to seek office.

The Dash

The dash has three main functions. It can be used to mark a sudden break in the flow of the writer's thought – to indicate, as it were, a dash towards another idea. Secondly, it can be used to introduce or set off a summary. In this function it is interchangeable with the colon, but the dash tends to be characteristic of a less formal style. Thirdly, double dashes can be used to set off a parenthetical element.

Examples:

I detest all clowns – but I exaggerate.
When I think of her –.
We assembled all our requirements – clothes, food, ropes, tools.
Bread, butter, jam – these were all on the table.
The leading conspirators – all but Brutus – were prepared to kill.

Parenthetical, supplementary and explanatory material can be set off by means of commas, dashes or brackets. There is a kind of descending order of relevance which indicates the most appropriate type of parenthesis marker. Commas are used to separate elements which are closely connected with the main idea expressed in the sentence. One would, for example, use commas as in this sentence. Double dashes are used where commas – to continue with this form of exemplar – would be too mild, and even confusing. While the choice of dash or comma is, for the main part, a stylistic matter, it is a safe rule that dashes should only be used where commas will not meet the purpose.

Brackets are the strongest separators of parentheses. They are used to mark off an element (or a whole sentence) which is intended to be seen separately by the reader. (Square brackets, incidentally, are printers' symbols, used to set off interpolated information not provided by the author. For example: 'During those years [1939–1942] Britain stood alone'.)

The Hyphen

The hyphen is a punctuation mark applied to single lexical items. It is used variously to form compound words. Some words begin life as hyphenated compounds but gradually assume the shape of a solid word: examples are *firearms, postman, football*. Opinions differ as to whether hyphenation should be preserved or abandoned in particular items. A number of lexicographers deprecate the modern trend to dispense with hyphens in such compounds as *liedetector, deathwatch, halfbaked, highwater,* while others insist that the hyphens are unnecessary even in such compounds as *waterpolo, washingmachine, houseagent*. In newspapers the words *to-day* and *to-morrow* are often still hyphenated, though most people write them solid. Hyphens are still necessary for compounds of words which are not usually joined, such as *a never-to-be-forgotten experience* or a *know-nothing* expression. Many writers hyphenate terms like *well-worn, well-intentioned,* but we would normally not hyphenate where the first component of the compound is an adverb (thus *slightly damaged, reddish green*) or where the words follow the noun: *the wall was well covered*. Hyphens are still almost universally used in number compounds (but only for those from twenty-one to ninety-nine) and in prefixed compounds: *ex-minister, self-appointed, all-round, re-created, semi-circular*.

The Apostrophe

The apostrophe is still regarded as necessary to indicate the possessive and contractions, despite the efforts of reformers like G. B. Shaw. The rules for signalling possession in animate nouns are easily learned. Some pupils, however, mislearn the rules to the extent of using apostrophes to indicate simple plurals. A common error is to confuse the possessive – for example, *its, yours, hers* – with such contractions as *it's*. Shaw's habit of using the apostrophe only where it is necessary to signal possession has much to commend it, as there is little danger of misconstruing forms like *dont, didnt, isnt* and so on. If the apostrophe is to be used in these forms, it must be used in the correct place – *isn't*, not *is'nt*.

Conclusion

In this chapter I have described the various sets of language skills required for efficient communication. All these skills flow from the general communicative competence developed during the first five to ten years of life. The basic, and most neglected, school skill is talk – using language for oral discourse. Talk ought to precede and accompany reading and writing activities, and reading and writing ought themselves to be associated in most kinds of lesson. Writing English, with its supplementary requirements of spelling and punctuation, is best developed in live, active situations in which motivation is high. Parents can help their children best by giving them a rich linguistic environment – full of engaging talk, reading-together activities and writing for fun. Any adult can further his own grasp of reading and writing techniques by paying attention to some fairly simple generalizations about these features of communication and by recognizing a few principles and rules. In this chapter I have presented both a number of observations about the nature of the different forms of communication and a number of rules which should be known. Conscious attention to rules, however, is ineffectual if not accompanied by persevering practice in the various communicative acts.

CHAPTER 4

Grammar, Rhetoric and Diction

Introduction

As I said in the introduction to Chapter 1, most teachers nowadays prefer to avoid unnecessary teaching of grammar. It is impossible, however, to avoid grammar altogether in the English lesson. Whether he knows it or not, every teacher employs and transmits grammatical concepts and terms. You cannot talk about English in any form – reading, writing, style, history – without using terms like *word, noun, sentence*. School grammar has had a long and troubled history, and it is often rightly said that much of what is taught is inaccurate and time-wasting. In this Chapter I discuss the history, status and purposes of school grammar and then offer a short, selective *grammar of the English sentence* concentrating on the structure of what is called the formal Standard English Sentence. The grammar presented here is all relevant to the job of constructing good sentences, and the next section describes the principles of sentence-composing. Good writing requires some knowledge of how to construct a paragraph, so I offer some guidance on the rhetoric of the paragraph. Another essential feature of good written English is selecting the right words for the intended effect: the chapter ends, therefore, with a section on diction.

School Grammar

In Chapter 1 I gave a brief account of the grammatical system which operates in a language. This was a view of grammar as a statement of how we order the symbols of language to form meaningful utterances. In this sense, a *grammar* is a description of how a language works. Historically, the word *grammar* has been used in various senses. In the Middle Ages it was taken to mean all classical writings – history, oratory, literature of all kinds. Scholars were said to be students of grammar when they studied the whole linguistic apparatus of a people. In the popular mind *grammar* is usually taken to mean what is 'correct' in speech and in writing. 'Bad grammar' means various kinds of error, of which some are deviant forms of syntax, some are better described as departures from established conventions of usage, and some are merely instances of different styles of address.

Traditional English grammar developed from the study of Greek and Latin scholars. The Greek grammar of Dionysius Thrax and the Latin grammar of Aelius Donatus and Priscian were used by British scholars to describe the structures of English from the sixteenth to the early twentieth centuries, and a large number of grammatical dissertations were published, offering different versions of the 'rules' of composing sentences in English. In his *Ars Grammatica* (written about 400 AD) Donatus had described Latin in terms of eight *partes orationis,* parts of the sentence, but the English grammarians mistranslated the phrase to mean 'eight parts of speech', and they applied these indiscriminately to their own language, believing that these grammatical categories were universal features of language. In the eighteenth and nineteenth centuries grammarians such as Joseph Priestley, Robert Lowth, George Campbell, Lindley Murray and Alexander Bain assumed that the grammatical structure of languages embodied universally valid rules of logic, and that Latin was of all languages the most logical. In their studies of English they set out to discover logical rules of syntax and usage, and naturally they based their rules of English on Latin models. They applied to English Latin grammatical concepts such as *tense, case* and *voice,* but failed to perceive that English and Latin are very different languages in their structural organization.

Using the Latinate grammars compiled for English, French, German and other European languages, nineteenth-century scholars wrote grammars for 'newly discovered' languages in Asia and Africa and South America. By the beginning of the twentieth century they had amassed many volumes of technical information, and early in the century three great grammars were produced: Henrik Poutsma's *Grammar of Late Modern English,* Etsko Kruisinga's *Handbook of Present-Day English,* and Otto Jespersen's *Modern English Grammar on Historical Principles.* But these were not *school* grammars. A school grammar is a compendium of rules and examples illustrating various aspects of the structure of the language designed to help pupils understand how words are put together to convey meaning.

The school grammars drawn from the traditional corpus of English grammatical scholarship tended to concentrate on two procedures: the parsing of words and the analysis of sentences. The verb *parse* derives from the Latin noun *pars,* 'part' of speech. Each of the eight parts of speech was defined *notionally,* in terms of its generalized meaning and function. Thus a *noun* was 'the name of an

object, person or thing', a *verb* was a 'doing word', an adjective a
'describing word', and so on. This notional manner of defining
words is not satisfactory for English. The differences between the
grammatical systems of Latin and English make it very difficult to
describe English by means of Latin categories.

Consider the string:
   girl room there this be in many full beauty.
These are all root items, but this is not a meaningful sentence. Grammar makes it meaningful by employing three organizing principles:
distribution (or word-ordering), agglutination, and inflection.
Ordering the words brings us to the string:
   there be many beauty full girl in this room.
Agglutination, which is the putting together of units to form new units, brings us to:
   there be many beautiful girl in this room.
Inflection, which is changing units to form new items, brings us to:
   there are many beautiful girls in this room.
English uses some agglutination and some inflection; but above all
English uses distribution. This is so commonplace a principle that we
tend not to notice it. The English speaker will 'correct for sequence',
for example accepting the string:
   the masters teaches the boy
to mean 'the master teaches the boy' rather than 'the boy teaches the
masters'. We would never think that the writer had made a correct
number agreement of noun and verb and used an incorrect word
order. But in some highly inflected languages the inflections would
be predominant signals. The Latin string:
   magistri pueros docet
is meaningless whatever the word-order, because the subject-noun
and the verb do not agree.

It would be hard to find two languages more unlike grammatically
than Latin and English, and although this is in itself a good reason
for teaching Latin to abler pupils it is not a good reason for basing
English grammars on Latin grammars. Latin has a tri-partite part of
speech system: stems inflected to show that they are verbs and stems
inflected to show that they are adjectives. English does not consistently use inflection to show that a word is any particular part of speech.
(It is true that we use some inflection: for example, *-able* and *-ful*
signal adjectives, *-ly* signals adverbs, *-s* signals plurality and so on.) In
English, words are not *by themselves* signalled as nouns, verbs and so
on. We use word-order to show what part of speech a word is. For
example, by themselves, the words *wash* or *end* cannot be identified as

noun or verb, but in phrases such as *wash the end* or *end the wash* you can easily label them.

In English, we can only distinguish between various classes of words in terms of their function in given sentences. Here are examples of some of the principal categories:

N	*blackness*
A	*beautiful*
V	*beautify*
NV	*walk, love, cure*
NA	*human, French, red*
AV	*clean, dry, end, wash, thin*
NAV	*fancy, faint, black, yellow*

That is only the beginning of a list of separate categories of English words – in this case words which operate variously as nouns, verbs and adjectives. You could add an infinite number of words to each list, but English words do not fit easily into single categories. Rather than classifying English words as parts of speech we should think of them as having *patterns of use*, or skills, of different kinds.

The Greeks and Romans, having highly inflected languages, assumed that a word's function and its meaning were nearly identical, so they defined their parts of speech in terms of meaning. When they teach pupils that a noun is the name of something and a verb is an action or state, teachers are still equating function and meaning. But this is not a satisfactory way of defining English words. For example, *dictation* is really an action, but it is a noun; *blue* is the name of a colour, but it is mostly an adjective; and we could go on multiplying instances of mismatching of this kind. The fact is that meaning is too vague a criterion for defining English words. Children should learn that words have functions – jobs to do in the sentence. In modern schools the study of English grammar is basically the study of English sentences, a study which sets out to determine how words work together to convey meaning. In linguistic terms, as we have seen in Chapter 1, grammar comprises syntax and morphology, but for pedagogical purposes it is syntax – the structure of the sentence – that pupils need to be taught.

The school grammar that emerged from the traditional scholarship of the eighteenth and nineteenth centuries tended to concentrate attention on the type of sentence found in formal, scholarly written English – the kind of writing done by historians such as Gibbon and Macaulay or litterateurs like Dr Johnson and Matthew Arnold. These sentences were classified as simple, compound, complex and compound–complex, in accordance with the mixture of main (or independent) and subordinate (or dependent) clauses contained in the sentence. A main clause was a string which could be considered 'a complete thought': when standing alone, therefore, it was a sentence e.g. The boy saw the dog. A sentence containing only one main clause was a *simple sentence*. A *compound sentence* contained two or more main clauses e.g. The boy saw the dog and the dog saw the boy. A *complex sentence* contained one main clause and one or more subordinate clauses e.g. The boy saw the dog, which was very large. A *compound–complex sentence* contained two or more main clauses and one or more subordinate clauses e.g. The boy saw the dog, which was very large, and the dog saw the boy. Note that this method of classifying sentences presupposes that the simple *sentence* itself can be defined as a complete thought. For ordinary purposes – for instance for controlling punctuation – this notion of a sentence is good enough. For the objective study of sentence grammar, however, it is not useful. If a simple sentence is a complete thought, a compound sentence must be two complete thoughts. But how do you decide what is a complete thought? The traditional school grammar is a mixture of categories, some deriving from one's intuitive apprehension of meaning and some deriving from functions. The sentence as perceived in this grammar is an entity which depends for its validity entirely on subjective meaning, while the clauses are functional categories dependent on this somewhat vague conception.

This dependence on intuition and subjective meaning earned severe criticism from the scholars who developed the theories and techniques of structural linguistics during the middle decades of the this century. They argued that a grammar based on Latin would not be valid for English since it is a very different language. They criticized the traditional scholars' exclusive concern with formal written English, arguing that the main substance of the language was spoken and that a grammar must be able to describe how the language actually works in practice. They criticized the traditional grammarians for their preoccupation with 'correctness' and with prescriptive (and proscriptive) 'rules'. Above all, they rejected the traditional grammarians' reliance on intuition and subjective meaning, arguing that grammar must be 'scientific' with demonstrable operating principles and objectively testable rules.

Structural linguists produced new grammars of English and other languages. Grammatical descriptions of English were produced by C. C. Fries, Harold Whitehall, Paul Roberts and other American linguists and by Randolph Quirk, Barbara Strang, W. H. Mittens and others in Britain. Some of these offered a considerable revision of the grammatical terminology of the traditionalists; Whitehall, Roberts and Mittins, in particular, proposed novel terms and techniques for use in schools.[57] M. A. K. Halliday's 'scale and category' grammar has contributed substantially to education in Britain, Australia and elsewhere, but no school grammar emerging from it has been popularized.

The school grammars developed from Chomsky's transformational-generative grammar have reverted in significant measure to the theoretical framework – and to some extent the terminology – of traditional grammar. TG, as it is called, accepts that intuition is essential to one's understanding of one's mother tongue, and the new grammarians readily employ inuitive judgments in their teaching. They also accept that a language may have discoverable logic – though not the same kind as the traditionalists inferred – and they agree that traditional grammar was, by and large, founded on valid theoretical substance.

The main purpose of teaching grammar in school must be to help the pupil to write effectively in English. Whether or not the teaching of grammar does fulfil this purpose has never been resolved. During the 1920s and 1930s in England there were many pedagogical objections to the role and status accorded grammar in the schools. By 1950 most progressive educators were convinced that it was largely a waste of time. Research work showed that there was no transfer of training from the study of grammar to the pupils' productive language work. On the other hand, the school grammar being thus condemned was mostly a mess of dull, unprofitable exercises such as the correction of 'common errors', minimal assertions and unsubstantiated 'rules' of composition and prosody – taught, moreover, by teachers who themselves had but slender acquaintanceship with grammatical knowledge.

In the USA many leading educators took the view that grammar teaching was ineffectual because the 'grammar' itself was poor stuff and the teachers lamentably ignorant.[58] If grammar was made a relevant and interesting study, it was argued, it would be an invaluable support to good writing and a source of insights into human behaviour. Much American research has thrown doubt on the efficacy of grammar teaching for improving communication skills, but the majority of teachers cling to the belief that it has value for this purpose. In Scotland, as in the USA, there was an upsurge of interest in 'new grammar' during the 1960s, accompanied by uncertainty as to whether it did the pupils any good. The consensus among leading educators was that the time spent traditionally on grammar could be better spent on productive training in reading and writing.[59] At the same time, teachers all over the world continue to rely on grammar lessons to provide their pupils with necessary concepts and terms for understanding the structure of sentences. If for no other reason than that terminology is needed for talking about pupils' composition, some grammar teaching is inescapable in the classroom. The best way of providing grammatical knowledge to pupils is by 'mention': from day to week to term, year by year, teachers should present information about the grammar of English *as the need arises* and *as the opportunity presents itself.* Slowly, an aggregation of insights and experiences will be built up in the pupil's mind, so that as he matures and learns he will be able to analyze the texture of his own and other people's writing, and to apply in practice the rules of grammar and rhetoric necessary for effective communication. Essential to this approach, of course, is that the teacher should have a thorough knowledge of grammar and rhetoric.

A Grammar of the English Sentence[60]

An English sentence is made up from combinations of *class words* and *function words.*

The class words are *nouns, verbs, adjectives, adverbs* and *pronouns.* These are members of an open inventory. They can be inflected (which means that a bound morpheme can be added to them): for example, *boy, boys; come, coming; small, smaller; lively, livelier.* (The pronoun is not an 'open class' word but it has other characteristics which make it a class word: for example it substitutes for a noun in many sentence frames; it can act as a headword in a phrase, and so on.)

The function words are members of closed systems. That is, there is a finite list of each group. There are five groups of function words:

  (i)   *Determiners:*   a, the, any, every, each, some; this, that, these, those; my, our, your, his, her, its, their. (They combine with nouns.)
  (ii) *Auxiliaries:*   will, may, have, can, must, do, should, might, be, etc. (They combine with verbs.)
  (iii) *Qualifiers:*   very, rather, quite, too, somewhat. (They combine with adjectives.)
  (iv) *Prepositions:* with, under, at, above, over, beside, in, etc. (They combine with nouns and noun phrases.)
  (v)   *Conjunctions:* and, or, but, nor, for, so. (They combine with class words, phrases and sentences.)

There are four classes of main verb. The verb *be* and its parts link words in a sentence:

They were sad. The girl is an actress. You are lying.

Intransitive verbs cannot be followed by nouns or adjectives:

> They slept. The girl acted. You lie.

Transitive verbs are normally followed by nouns:

> They made pancakes. The girl played a part. You tell a lie.

Copulative verbs are followed by adjectives or nouns:

> They seemed sad. The girl felt excited. She became my friend.

In a basic sentence each class word occupies its own typical position. The noun normally occupies the first position, the verb the second position. Thus the most basic sentence consists of a noun or pronoun followed by a verb:

> Men sleep. I go. Everyone eats.

The third place in a basic sentence may be occupied by a noun or adjective. A noun in the first position may be combined with one or more determiners or adjectives to form a *noun phrase*. A verb may be combined with an adverb or auxiliary or noun phrase to form a *verb phrase*. Thus we have a basic sentence structure consisting of a noun phrase followed by a verb phrase: NP + VP. In terms of *function* in the sentence, the NP occupying the first position is the *subject* and the VP following the NP is the predicator:

Subject NP	Predicator VP
The poor little boy	looked ill.
Boys	like fighting.
New York in the spring	seems alive.
John	gave his mother a kiss.
Everyone	sang.
Mrs Smith	came home yesterday.

Adverbial additions to a basic NP + VP modify the information given:

> Boys fight *frequently*. The little boy *sometimes* liked fighting. John gave his mother a kiss *yesterday*.

This adverbial function can be performed by a noun phrase preceded by a preposition:

> Boys like fighting *during play*. John gave his mother a kiss *on the cheek*. The little girl danced *behind the stage*.

Adverbials can be added in various positions:

> *Cheerfully*, John kissed his mother.
>
> John *cheerfully* kissed his mother.
>
> John kissed his mother *cheerfully*.

The NP can be qualified by adding adjectives, qualifiers and prepositional phrases. Thus the NP *the boy* can be expanded:

(i) By adjectives: the poor boy
                                       the poor little boy
(ii) By qualifiers + adjectives: the very poor boy
(iii) By prepositional phrases: the poor boy in the park
                                       the little boy with the limp

In a noun phrase the noun (or nominal) word is called the
headword (h) and the other words are *modifiers* (m):

m   m   m   h

the little brown jug

m   m   m   h

my dearest little love

m   m   m   h   m   m   m   h

the fat little girl (in the blue dress)

The basic sentence can be divided into four elements: Subject,
Predicator, Complement and Adjunct. The S place is occupied by a
NP. The P place is occupied by a VP. The C place is occupied by a
NP. The A place is occupied by adverbials.

S	P	C	A
The boys	dance		merrily.
London	is	my home	now.
Mr Smith	bought	the books.	

The Adjunct can occur in different positions:

A	S	P
Merrily	we	danced.

S	A	P	C
Mr Jones	with great presence of mind	closed	the door.

S	P	A	C
I	saw	with horror	what followed.

Basic sentences are transformed into other sentences by the
application of grammatical rules. The basic S + P declarative
sentence can be transformed into a *There* sentence, or into a com-

mand (or imperative) or question (interrogative).

For a *There* sentence, the rules require the placing of *be* or auxiliaries before the subject:

A boy was waiting at the corner.

There was a boy waiting at the corner.

The imperative transformation operates on basic sentences containing *you* in the subject position and the auxiliary *will*. The transformation deletes the subject and the auxiliary:

You will go home.

Go home!

Another transformation, which intensifies the command, retains the subject:

You, go home!

Since the word *you* can be too indefinite, we often employ a person's name for the transformation:

John, go home right away.

Yes-no interrogatives are formed by removing the auxiliary from the VP and putting it in front of the subject:

John is going away.

Is John going away?

The girl should have been with her mother.

Should the girl have been with her mother?

Other *yes-no* transformations require the use of the auxiliary *do*:

John likes her.

Does John like her?

Do or one of its parts is placed before the subject and the verb changes its tense-form. If the verb is in past-tense form, the past-tense form of *do* is required:

John liked her.

Did John like her?

Every man had his own weapon.

Did every man have his own weapon?

Declaratives containing a form of *have* can be transformed by transposing the verb:

Every man has his own weapon.

Has every man his own weapon?

Other interrogatives are formed by using a *wh-* word to transform a yes-no question:

The men elected a leader.

Did the men elect a leader?

When did the men elect a leader?

Someone was tapping at the window.
Was someone tapping at the window?
Who was tapping at the window?

Each boy held something.
Did each boy hold something?
What did each boy hold?

Basic sentences can be transformed into compound sentences by linking them with a coordinating conjunction:

The men elected Tom leader. He accepted the position.
The men elected Tom leader and he accepted the position.

The men wanted Jake as leader. He refused the invitation.
The men wanted Jake as leader, but he refused the invitation.

Each of the basic sentences making up the compound sentence is a *main clause*. Main clauses can be combined to form compound sentences in various ways:

(i) By conjunction:	I came, and I stayed.
(ii) By comma + conjunction:	I came, I saw her, and I stayed.
(iii) By semi-colon:	I came; I saw her; I stayed.
(iv) By semi-colon + transition-word:	I arrived late; nevertheless, I quickly began the task.

(Other transition-words are: *also, accordingly, besides, consequently, furthermore, moreover, hence, however, still, subsequently, then, therefore, thus.*)

Two basic sentences can be combined by making one a main clause and the other a phrase:

The boy went home. He was sick.
The boy, being sick, went home.

I hesitated. I could not understand.
Unable to understand, I hesitated.

Another way of combining two basic sentences is to make one a main clause and the other a subordinate clause beginning with a subordinating conjunction:

Main clause	Subordinate clause
I hesitated	because I could not understand.
The boys travelled	as soon as they could.
Mr Jones laughed	when he saw the car.
Everyone would be pleased	if you joined the party.
He came alone	so that we would not be afraid.
They would not work	unless they were paid.

These sentences, consisting of one main clause and one subordinate clause, are called *complex* sentences. A complex sentence can consist of a main clause with several subordinate clauses:

Main clause	Subordinate clause	Subordinate clause	Subordinate clause
He laughed	when he saw	that I had arrived	before he had written to me.

A *compound-complex* sentence consists of two or more main clauses with one or more subordinate clauses:

Subordinate clause	Main clause	Main clause	Subordinate clause
As soon as I saw him	I stopped	and he asked me	where I had been
Subordinate clause			
when he called.			

Complex sentences can sometimes be more economical in expression and consequently more effective, if phrases are used instead of subordinate clauses. One method is to use a *participial* phrase:

Mr Jones picked up the book and went into the house.

Participial phrase	Main clause
Picking up the book,	Mr Jones went into the house.

Because he was lame, my uncle seldom went out.

Participial phrase	Main clause
Being lame,	my uncle seldom went out.

After they had been interrogated, the prisoners were released.

Participial phrase	Main clause
Having been interrogated,	the prisoners were released.

Another device for reducing a subordinate clause to a phrase is the *infinitive* phrase:

He drove a long way so that he could talk to her.

Main clause	Infinitive phrase
He drove a long way	to talk to her.

In order to meet his obligation he worked the whole day.

Infinitive phrase	Main clause
To meet his obligation	he worked the whole day.

Another method is to use an *absolute* phrase:

As soon as the teacher had ended his talk the boys ran home.

Absolute phrase	Main clause
The teacher having ended his talk	the boys ran home.

Another type of transformation is to combine basic sentences by making one a main clause and the other a subordinate *adjectival* clause:

> This is the woman. I love her.
> This is the woman *I love*.
> This is the woman *whom I love*.

Adjectival clauses can be reduced to adjectival phrases for economy or effect:

> The girl who is sitting over there is my friend.
> The girl sitting over there is my friend.

> All the men who have been selected for examination should report to me.
> All the men selected for examination should report to me.

Rhetoric

The sentence grammar given in the last section is a mere selection of the information carried by a comprehensive grammar of English. My selection was designed to present some of the essential facts needed for an understanding of a written English sentence. Much of the grammar offered in academic studies of English is of little direct value to the native speaker, whose intuitions give him ample guidance as to the functions of words in the sentence. A certain amount of grammatical terminology, however, is unavoidable in discussion of the composition of English sentences.

Rhetoric is the art of composing effective prose. It has been defined as 'the art or talent by which discourse is adapted to its end'.[61] The Greeks and Romans much prized the rules and procedures of rhetoric laid down by Aristotle, Cicero and Quintilian. In Shakespeare's time elaborate schemes were available to the aspirant author. In the eighteenth and nineteenth centuries the work of rhetoricians such as Campbell, Kames, Blair, Whateley and Bain provided guidance on the practical criticism of published texts and consequently on the techniques of composition. In schools, however, the studies of the scholars tended to be reduced to the form of prescriptive, often ill-informed and ill-organized rules and exercises. Pupils were given no encouragement to write spontaneously or creatively, and since good writing can only result from much previous writing it was not surprising that school superintendents and inspectors kept on finding lamentable gaps between pupils' explicit knowledge of the 'rules' and their ability to write effectively. In recent decades there has been a revival of interest in rhetoric as the study of the composition of good English writing: expositions of the criteria of first-rate prose.

The beginning of rhetorical skill is control of the grammar of the sentence. The student who cannot construct a grammatically acceptable sentence will never be able to write effective English. Grammaticality, however, may be won by sacrificing fluency. If you are so concerned to write without grammatical error that you will not attempt sentences of any length or complexity, you will confine your discourse to dull, repetitious, stilted prose. If the student is to develop his writing skills, he must be aware of the variety of syntactic patterns available to him for the expression of any thought. This is *stylistic choice*, and rhetoric is the art of making stylistic decisions.

Grammaticality, for standard written English,* requires that each sentence should be constituted as explained in the previous section. A subordinate clause, or a phrase, cannot stand alone. The 'sentence fragment', as it is called, is a heinous sin in formal written English. Another conspicuous error is the 'comma splice', the linking of sentences by means of a comma and nothing else: for example, *The boy was young, he felt embarrassed.* Thus the use of conjunctions, semicolons and subordination is a prerequisite to acceptable formal writing. Another source of error is lack of *agreement*. A verb must agree in number with its subject. (*The man goes* not *The man go.*) A pronoun must agree in number with the noun or pronoun which antecedes it. (It is wrong to write *One must always remember their number in the army.*) Although the native speaker hardly ever makes mistakes in agreement in everyday discourse, it is not always easy to avoid error when writing more complex sentences. In the main, errors like the following are committed through carelessness, but they must be avoided for good writing:

> *The repetition of many sentence patterns give a dullness to your writing.*
> *John, as well as Mary and Tom, were selected.*
> *Neither John nor Tom were chosen.*
> *Along the street there was found seven empty cans.*
> *This is one of the coldest days that has been recorded.*
> *Each of the boys followed their friends.*
> *When a cat or a dog gets hurt, they want to hide.*
> *The nation does their best to keep the peace.*

Agreement in number can be difficult when the writer uses a 'noun of multitude' but fails to use it consistently. Here is an actual example of this error.[62]

* This section deals with the composition of standard written English. Standards vary for other forms of English, as we shall see in the next chapter.

Our client is a leading company in the automotive aftermarket business operating in the UK and world-wide. An important part of their sales promotion activity is the production of news media, majoring on three colourful and informative magazines. Through these our client keeps their UK and world-wide customers abreast of the company's activities.

Beyond the level of grammaticality the composing of effective sentences is a matter of making the most appropriate choices from among options which are all basically correct. Although we are now in the domain of style, for which it is not possible to lay down rules, we can at least apply some rhetorical principles. Most of these are concerned with preserving in the sentence the logicality and unity of the ideas which the writer wishes to convey. It is unlikely that a writer would deliberately use confusing sentence structures, even when he wishes to convey confusion or uncertainty.

Ideas should be related syntactically in order to be related logically. This relatedness should be immediately clear in the sentence. Thus ideas not logically connected – or where the connection might be unclear – should not be combined in the same sentence. For example, the ideas in the sentence *The study of Geography broadens the mind, and Johnson travelled through Europe* are not clearly related and should be in separate sentences.

Clarity is an important criterion in effective writing, and this need must govern a variety of decisions for sentence content. A sentence might be confusing because of excessive detail. For example, the sentence *In my childhood my father, a man of great enthusiasms, especially for hobbies like walking, birdwatching and nature study, used to take me and my sister Elizabeth, who was three years younger than me, walking along the river which passed by our house* is much too cluttered with detail. If these details are necessary (and only the writer is entitled to decide that) they should be given in some other form: in separate sentences, or in a compound–complex sentence with appropriate punctuation.

The art of sentence-making lies to a large extent in learning how to combine pairs of sentences by coordination or subordination. These techniques must be learned through experience and practice. A few simple principles can be learned by maturer students, however, and some practice will reinforce the skill. These may be summarized and exemplified as follows:

1. *Where there is a causal relationship between ideas, show it.*

    <u>Poor</u>: Mankind has eaten garlic for many centuries. It is used to flavour food. It is thought to have magic powers.

    <u>Better</u>. Mankind has eaten garlic for many centuries, not only for flavouring food but also because it is thought to have magic powers.

OR

Mankind has eaten garlic for many centuries, not only because it is good for flavouring food but also because it is thought to have magic powers.

2. *The main idea should be given as the main clause.*
Poor: Daniels defeated men much bigger than himself being less than average height and weight.
Better: Daniels defeated men much bigger than himself, despite being less than average height and weight.

OR

Although he was less than average height and weight, Daniels defeated men much bigger than himself.

3. *If you want to combine main ideas, build a compound sentence.*
Poor: Mankind has eaten garlic for many centuries. It is good for flavouring food. It is thought to have magic powers.
Better: Garlic is good for flavouring food, and it is thought to have magic powers: for these reasons mankind has eaten it for many centuries.

4. *Parallel ideas should be combined in parallel structures.*
Poor: Daniels had competed often that summer, also finding time to write newspaper stories.
Better: Daniels had competed often that summer, and had also found time to write newspaper stories.
Poor: He decided that he had passed the peak of his performance and to consider retiring before the end of the year.
Better: He decided that he had passed the peak of his performance and that he should consider retiring before the end of the year.

5. *Maintain the same point of view in the sentence.*
Poor: Daniels thought up the stories as he jogged along the country lanes, and at night they were written down in his notebook.
Better: Daniels thought up the stories as he jogged along the country lanes, and at night wrote them down in his notebook.
Poor: Gather the fruit as early as possible in the morning, and while fresh they should be dried and frozen.
Better: The fruit should be gathered as early as possible in the morning, and dried and frozen while still fresh.

6. *Emphasize important ideas by placing them in the most prominent positions, the beginning or the end of the sentence.*

Poor: Some species will not survive into the next century, if the slaughter continues.

Better: If the slaughter continues, some species will not survive into the next century.

Poor: Our two greatest statesmen met for the first time one sunny July day some years ago.

Better: One sunny July day some years ago, our two greatest statesmen met for the first time.

7. *Ensure that the meaning of the sentence is not distorted by the misplacement of a word, a phrase or a clause.*

Poor: It was reported that over a million people play golf in Canada.

Better: It was reported that in Canada over a million people play golf.

Poor: Having spent his whole career in journalism, you would expect Carlson to know a split infinitive when he sees one.

Better: You would expect that Carlson, having spent his whole career in journalism, would know a split infinitive when he sees one.

Poor: I should welcome information about the writer John Jamieson who died in 1843 to aid my research.

Better: I should welcome information to aid my research about the writer John Jamieson who died in 1843.

OR

To aid my research I should welcome information about the writer John Jamieson, who died in 1843.

Poor: Strapped to her leg, the police officer found a smuggled weapon.

Better: The police officer found a smuggled weapon strapped to her leg.

Poor: The company has invested heavily in a new oilfield which was discovered looking for natural gas.

Better: The company has invested heavily in a new oilfield which was discovered during a search for natural gas.

Poor: A recipe for marmalade caught my eye, which requires honey instead of sugar.

Better: My eye caught a recipe for marmalade which requires honey instead of sugar.

Poor: An ignorant fool, I have no respect for him.

Better: I have no respect for him: he is an ignorant fool.

Poor: Every year the firemen attend hundreds of fires, and every year thousands of people die as a result.

Better: Every year the firemen attend hundreds of fires, as a result of which thousands of people die.

OR

Every year the firemen attend hundreds of fires; as a result of these fires thousands of people die.

8. *Ensure that the sentence is unambiguous.*

Poor: The council decided to build cheap modern apartments.

Better: The council decided to build modern low-rent apartments.

OR

The council decided to build cheaply a block of modern apartments.

Poor: The chairman remarked that in the circumstances the society could not employ a better secretary.

Better: The chairman remarked that in the circumstances the secretary employed had proved excellent.

The following extract from the minutes of a borough council meeting illustrates the sometimes hilarious ambiguity that English can present.[63]

Councillor Trafford took exception to the proposed notice at the entrance of South Park: 'No dogs must be brought to this park except on a lead.' He pointed out that this order would not prevent an owner from releasing his pets, or pet, from a lead when once safely inside the Park!

The Chairman (Colonel Vine): What alternative wording would you propose, Councillor?

Councillor Trafford: 'Dogs are not allowed in this Park without leads.'

Councillor Hogg: Mr Chairman, I object. The order should be addressed to the owners, not to the dogs.

Councillor Trafford: That is a nice point. Very well then: 'Owners of dogs are not allowed in this Park unless they keep them on leads.'

Councillor Hogg: Mr Chairman, I object. Strictly speaking, this would prevent me as a dog-owner from leaving my dog in the back-garden at home and walking with Mrs Hogg across the Park.

Councillor Trafford: Mr Chairman, I suggest that our legalistic friend be asked to redraft the notice himself.

Councillor Hogg: Mr Chairman, since Councillor Trafford finds it so difficult to improve on my original wording, I accept. 'Nobody without his dog on a lead is allowed in this Park.'

Councillor Trafford: Mr Chairman, I object: this reads as if it were a general injunction to the Borough to lead their dogs into the Park.

Councillor Hogg interposed a remark for which he was called to order; upon his withdrawing it, it was directed to be expunged from the Minutes.

The Chairman: Councillor Trafford, Councillor Hogg has had three tries; you have had only two . . .
Councillor Trafford: 'All dogs must be kept on leads in this Park.'
The Chairman: I see Councillor Hogg rising quite rightly to raise another objection. May I anticipate him with another amendment: 'All dogs in this Park must be kept on the lead.'

This draft was put to the vote and carried unanimously, with two abstentions.

Beyond the sentence, rhetoric deals with the structure of paragraphs. The Scottish logician, Alexander Bain, asserted that a paragraph should be an 'expanded' sentence: a group of sentences containing a theme or topic laid down in a 'key' sentence and developed in supporting sentences. The notion that every paragraph must contain a key or topic sentence was never borne out by study of established writers' paragraphing, so the teachers proposed that the topic sentence might be 'implied' or 'dispersed' over a number of sentences. The truth is, however, that there is no organic connection between a sentence and a paragraph. Such assertions as 'a paragraph is to a sentence what a sentence is to a word' and 'the paragraph seems to be only a macro-sentence' betray a poor understanding of the way in which a writer controls his paragraphing.[64]

A paragraph ending signals a pause to the reader. In prose fiction a paragraph might end when the writer wishes to introduce dialogue, or when he wants to switch the reader's attention to another character, or another scene. Since the paragraph break signals a pause, paragraphs tend to be shorter in prose written for children or readers who prefer light, easy-to-read matter. In expository writing, the paragraph break usually signals the completion of one stage of the writer's discourse. Since discourse, in the sense of 'message' or 'argument', must be presented in sequences, one stage or flow leading to another, paragraphing gives the writer some control over the reader's rate of absorption of the meaning.

Since he is conscious all the time he is writing of this need to put limits on the flow of his exposition, the writer relates the paragraph to the structure that is greater than itself, not to the sentences that it contains. This 'macro-structure' varies with the kind of writing: it is a chapter of a novel, a chapter or sub-chapter of a scholarly work, an essay or an article. Obviously the authorial decisions made about the macro-structure are the main influences brought to bear on the length and structure of the paragraph. 'Paragraph structure is part and parcel of the structure of the discourse as a whole . . . Paragraphs are not composed; they are discovered.'[65]

When all this has been said, however, it remains true that a good writer will pay close attention to the linkage of sentences within the paragraph. The decision to break off and begin a new paragraph is not an arbitrary one, nor is it arrived at intuitively. Even if he is not conscious of so doing, an efficient writer will be monitoring his sentence flow as it appears on the page, fitting the structures of both sentences and paragraphs to the inherent structure of his discourse: that is, the structure he intends to impose on it, or the structure that he feels is being imposed on it by the trend of his thinking.

These skills cannot be taught by prescription. The examination of good models, which show how accomplished writers have managed the presentation of their thoughts and feelings, can be highly efficacious if the teacher is skilled and the pupil capable of profiting by the experience. The best learning context, however, is where the student and teacher work together, in some contrived fashion, to try various techniques. The student-writer and the teacher-reader can, of course, be the same person. Robert Louis Stevenson's confession, 'I have thus played the sedulous ape to Hazlitt, to Lamb, to Wordsworth', is worth taking as an injunction. 'Where there is much desire to learn', wrote Milton in *Areopagitica*, 'there of necessity will be much arguing, much writing, many opinions'. Rhetoric, the art of composing, cannot be separated from all the other forms and activities of communication. The effective teacher will ensure that they occur together.

Diction

Diction is that part of the composition process concerned with the choice of words. It is obviously of little use to be able to construct well-formed sentences if their meaning is not well conveyed; and it is the meaning of the class words which carry the main semantic burden in a sentence.

Those who find more than the usual difficulty in putting pen to paper may as often as not be literally at a loss for words. Of course, everyone meets with difficulty in composing at some level; people who are fluent in one subject may be slow and diffident in another, finding it hard to seize upon the words which seem to express the thoughts struggling to escape the mind. Granted that we do most, if not all, of our thinking *in* words, there is always a choice to be made at the point of utterance. What Wordsworth called 'choice words, and measured phrase' do not come easily.

The only effective way to acquire a good vocabulary is to read and listen extensively and to reinforce one's grasp of words by using them in writing and talking. Even so most people tend to acquire vocabulary within certain areas of interest; we build up a number of specialized lexicons. The most 'common' topical contexts, those like politics, the arts and popular science, are dealt with in the better newspapers – journalists are the most powerful unacknowledged educators in the world. Students can do more for each other's learning by exchanging chat about what the Sunday papers say than they would ever realize. Those exercises in textbooks and articles in popular magazines which purport to 'Increase Your Word-Power' do no more than present arbitrary tests: rote-learning of word-lists is largely a waste of time. The stereotype of the 'swot' in school stories – the bespectacled boy or girl who keeps 'trying out' long words – is, in fact, an example that all young people should be encouraged to follow. Experimenting with words you have newly picked up is one way of assimilating them.

Every student should have a good dictionary by his side as he reads, so that he can look up any word which is new to him. Referring to the dictionary must become a habit, for it is easy to do without it. Most of the time an efficient reader can deduce a word's meaning from its context, but this by itself will not guarantee that the word and its meaning will be remembered.

Another useful reference book which is worth having by you, especially when writing, is a thesaurus. This is a reference list of words and related items, such as synonyms, antonyms, and associated phrases. Because of its multivariate origins, English is rich in synonyms, and this very wealth was long ago recognized to be a source of confusion for the young. The dictionary produced by Henry Cockeram in 1623 had some of the characteristics of a thesaurus and was designed to give the reader 'the exact and ample word' to express a meaning.[66] The most famous of all thesauri is that of Peter Mark Roget's, published in 1852 and still being issued. The thesaurus is an aid to rhetorical competency because it provides an inventory of words which have semantic behaviours similar to the one the writer has in mind. Frequently, in the act of composing, you have a word 'at the tip of your tongue', but, firstly, you are unable to express it and secondly you are not all sure if it is the word you really need in any case. The thesaurus acts as a trigger to a series of words, one of which may be the one you were seeking. Alternatively, the thesaurus may suggest a word which is new to you but which happens to be the most appropriate word for the context.

A danger presented by the thesaurus is that not every word listed may be exactly right for the context you wish to furnish. To use a word that is not apt is a stylistic error: it fails to convey your meaning, and if it is conspicuously inapt it will 'interfere' with your communication by making the reader react unfavourably to you as a writer.

The use of words incorrectly has long been a cause for ridicule. Mrs Malaprop, in Sheridan's *The Rivals*, who tells her niece to 'illiterate' her lover from her memory, was the original perpetrator of the malapropism:

> 'I would by no means wish a daughter of mine to be a progeny of learning; I don't think so much learning becomes a young woman: for instance, I would never let her meddle with Greek, or Hebrew, or algebra, or simony, or fluxions, or paradoxes, or such inflammatory branches of learning – neither would it be necessary for her to handle any of your mathematical, astronomical, diabolical instruments. But, Sir Anthony, I would send her, at nine years old, to a boarding-school, in order to learn a little ingenuity and artifice. Then, sir, she should have a supercilious knowledge of accounts; – and as she grew up, I would have her instructed in geometry, that she might know something of the contagious countries; – but above all, Sir Anthony, she should be mistress of orthodoxy, that she might not mis-spell, and mis-pronounce words so shamefully as girls usually do; and likewise that she might reprehend the true meanig of what she is saying.'

The malapropism is still endemic in our newspapers. Within the last two years the following examples have been recorded:*

'they acquainted themselves creditably' (acquitted)
'replete with family' (complete)
'strangely reticent' (reluctant)
'refreshing and enervating' (stimulating)
'gathering her voluptuous skirts' (voluminous)
'the bus-like discomfiture of the seats' (discomfort)
'to flaunt the strict conventions of Chinese life' (flout)
'the cathedral close remains outside the purloins of the conservation area' (purlieus)
'the Ottawa delegate's plaintiff appeal' (plaintive)
'one factor which will mitigate against the effects' (militate)
'just the anecdote to a gloomy summer day' (antidote)

It is only too easy to use words incorrectly, especially when one writes hastily; that explains why so many mistakes of this kind are found in journalists' writing. The only way to prevent oneself falling into error thus is to develop the habit of self-monitoring as one writes and, if possible, to make time to check one's writing before sending it away.

One of the most common rhetorical weaknesses in English prose writing is the excessive use of hackneyed expressions or clichés.

* In the 'This English' column of the *New Statesman*.

George Orwell described this as 'gumming together long strips of words which have already been set in order by someone else'.[67] There is a difference, however, between using commonplace idioms, which we all do every day because this is a normal part of ordinary intercourse, and writing prose which is conspicuously cliché-ridden. In a casually dictated business letter, or a scribbled memorandum on a technical matter, one would naturally use the familiar linguistic tokens normal in these circumstances. It is only when one is consciously aiming to write for effect that one should make an effort to avoid what Geoffrey Leech has called 'the mechanical, humdrum, repetitive element in everyday communication'.[68]

Every cliché, it is worth remembering, began life as a smart remark. Sam Slick, a character created in 1835 by a Canadian writer, Thomas Chandler Haliburton, gave us 'raining cats and dogs', 'quick as a wink', 'seeing is believing' and other expressions which are now common currency. The metaphorical force in expressions like these has drained away with time, and while they do not lend sparkle to our conversation neither do they attract attention. The cliché to avoid is the one that the reader *notices*, the expression that causes interference in communication because the reader thinks about the language rather than the meaning. This kind of cliché is vividly illustrated in Frank Sullivan's 'The Cliché Expert':[69]

Q. Mr Arbuthnot, as an expert in the use of the cliché, are you prepared to testify here today regarding its application in topics of sex, love, matrimony, and so on?
A. I am, Mr Sullivan.
Q. Very good. Now, Mr Arbuthnot, what's love?
A. Love is blind.
Q. Good. What does love do?
A. Love makes the world go round.
Q. Whom does a young man fall in love with?
A. With the Only Girl in the World.
Q. Whom does a young woman fall in love with?
A. With the Only Boy in the World.
Q. When do they fall in love?
A. At first sight.
Q. How?
A. Madly.
Q. They are then said to be?
A. Victims of Cupid's darts.
Q. And he?
A. Whispers sweet nothings in her ear.
Q. Who loves a lover?
A. All the world loves a lover.

The only general principle of diction that can be offered the writer in English is that the selection of vocabulary should be governed by one's feeling for style. Style is a feature of writing which is impossible to describe briefly: many volumes have been written over three centuries in a long struggle to explicate this term. Every piece of writing is executed with a certain mode of expression. In so far as the right style has been struck by the writer, the language successfully conveys not only the raw 'information' but also the undertones of which the writer wants the reader to be aware. Of all the hundreds of words he might use in a particular context, the successful writer uses a selection which, he hopes, will fulfil his intentions. To achieve this end he must be thoroughly aware of such aspects of language as *variety, register, style* and *appropriateness*, all of which will be dealt with in the next chapters.

Conclusion

In this chapter I have attempted to provide a necessarily brief account of what is meant by grammar, rhetoric and diction. An understanding of the grammatical make-up of the English sentence is essential to be able to write good formal English, and I have presented a short, highly selective grammar in order to identify the main features of the sentence. On this basis I have suggested a number of rhetorical principles, pit-falls to be avoided, and guides to reassure the student writer. In the section on diction I have confined my attention to a few of the more common aspects of that most difficult of tasks, choosing the right words.

CHAPTER 5

The Englishes of the World

Introduction

The English language is so varied, with so many different forms of
the language spoken in different ways, that it is difficult to understand why people think of it as *a language* at all. In fact, it is the standard variety of the language spoken in their own geographical area
that people think of as 'English'. Thus Americans sometimes refer to
'speaking American' and most English people mean 'English
English' when they refer to the language. To understand the nature
of the English language it is necessary to know about the varieties of
the language and how they are related to each other. The more you
know about this the more you will realize that 'standards' are more
difficult to define than most people think.

Dialects

Educators concerned with the techniques of teaching young people
to use their mother tongue efficiently tend to think of English as a
whole, single language. My account of English grammar and rhetoric
is written from that point of view – on the assumption that *formal
written standard English* is the target behaviour in learning English. In
fact, however, English consists of many sub-varieties of the language.
In any one English-speaking country there will be groups of people
who each speak a kind of English that is distinctive because of certain
phonological, grammatical and lexical habits preferred by members
of the group. Such a variety is called a *dialect*. Like all widely established languages, English consists of a number of dialects.

Students of language have long known that the language we use is
related in various ways to the situations in which we use it. It was this
awareness of the situational associations of language that lay behind
the rhetorics of the Greeks and Romans, rhetoric for them being the
art of manipulating the situation by means of language – the art of
persuasion. Shakespeare's keen awareness of this characteristic of
language is evident in his clever juxtaposition of different styles of ad-

dress, for example in *Julius Caesar* where he makes Mark Antony's speech to the mob more rhetorically effective than Brutus's more prosaic explanations.

Shakespeare was also aware that every individual speaker has a set of linguistic habits which, put together, form a distinct language variety unique to that individual. Nowadays this personal language repertoire is called an *idiolect*. An individual's idiolect exhibits his experience in life: where he was brought up, how he was educated, what he does for a living, how he uses his spare time, and so on. Theoretically, it should be possible for a trained linguist to listen to a sample of anyone's speech and do the kind of party trick that Professor Higgins does in *Pygmalion* or *My Fair Lady*, identifying the birthplace, dwelling place and schooling of the speaker. In practice, however, too little is known about dialects to allow more than comparatively gross guesswork. At the same time, any mature speaker of English can quickly identify these broad facts about a stranger. Even a child can immediately detect the 'strangeness' of a person speaking a different dialect.

An individual's idiolect, however, can comprise features of more than one dialect. Many Scots, for example, like many Germans, can operate competently in one dialect (Standard Scots English) during the day and in a very different dialect (Scots) at weekends or holidays, putting on the local dialect, as it were, with their casual garments. An idiolect also contains features, such as words and grammatical conventions, which originate in the social milieu of the speaker, current or past. It contains, also, phonological features, mostly habits of articulation and accent, which derive from the various speechways one has been part of throughout life. Because these features are numerous and are acquired in different measures and in different permutations, no individual's language-using profile is identical with another's. Hence the term *idiolect*, meaning the uniquely personal set of language features possessed by any one individual.

There are at least four kinds of dialect to be identified in English.[70] One kind, which is of interest only to scholars, is the *temporal* dialect, the variety of English characteristic of a given historical period. Obviously a temporal dialect of English will have dialectal dimensions related to social and geographical characteristics. A *geographical* dialect is a variety of the language which possesses features resulting from the life of a community in a particular region or country. A *social* dialect is a variety which displays features resulting from the social status of a group of people and all the associated habits of life and outlook of that group. It is again obvious that geographical and social dialectal features will not be completely distinguishable from one another. In using these terms we are using abstractions to enable us to make broad general observations about language. It may be useful to speak of, for instance, a middle-class Scots dialect, or a lower-class South London dialect, but it is important to remember that such descriptions must be extremely general and crude because the individuals ascribed to any one group all employ their own idiolects. A dialect might be thought of as a set of idiolects peculiar to a place or social group, but it would be more accurate to think of it as a set of broadly distinctive features of idiolects.

A fourth kind of English dialect has only two categories: Standard and non-Standard. Standard English is the dialect one has in mind when talking about 'correct' English. All the rules contained in school textbooks on grammar and composition are rules of Standard English – or SE to use the standard abbreviation. SE is the most prestigious dialect of English throughout the world. It is the descendant of the East Midland dialect that emerged towards the end of the fourteenth century as the standard speech of London and of the royal court.[71] Written English developed mainly from this dialect, partly because the region included the universities of Oxford and Cambridge but more importantly because it was the language of commerce, law and government in London. The introduction of printing in 1450 established this dialect as the standard throughout most of England. By Shakespeare's time the distinction between what came to be called Polite English and Vulgar English was well established, and few people south of the Scottish border were taught to write a different variety. A standard literary English had developed, though many spoken dialects survived, as indeed is still the case.

Standard English is characterized by the fact that it is the dialect understood by all educated speakers of the language. Wherever English is taught in schools, it is SE that provides both the medium and the matter of instruction. Wherever English is written for transactional purposes it is SE that is used. SE is perhaps better described as *standardized* English, for it is the product of normalization, the trend towards uniformity characteristic of institutions such as governments, armed services, commercial enterprises and other bodies in which large-scale communication is necessary. To enlist a student into the larger community of a nation it is necessary to incorporate his idiolect in the linguistic norms that give the community its identity; throughout the English-speaking world this means teaching SE.

SE has nothing to do with accent. Speakers of SE in different parts of the world speak it with very different habits of articulation and acoustic features such as pronunciation, though the grammar may be much the same. People tend to confuse dialect and accent because certain accents have been accorded social prestige in some countries. In England, particularly, the phonological features of SE as spoken in the English public schools and older universities has been used by linguists to represent the standard. Known as RP (Received Pronunciation) this variety of speech is used technically to provide norms for the purpose of making phonetic analyses of English. It is also the speech variety commonly employed by newsreaders and announcers in British radio and television. RP should not be confused with SE. It does not represent the phonology of SE in any other part of the world. There is a Standard Scots English, a Standard Welsh English, a Standard Australian English, some variations of which may be equivalent to RP in that they are perceived by many people as the accent of privilege or social superiority. Dialect includes accent as one of its features, but accent and dialect are not the same thing.

Contrasting with SE is non-Standard English. In every English-speaking community there are various forms of non-Standard English spoken alongside SE. All geographical dialects are, by definition, non-Standard, but there may be striking internal diversities due to social dialectal features. Social non-Standard dialects exist in all the major languages: High German, Parisian French, Florentine Italian and Moscow Russian are all well-known terms, and in all of these cases there are social as well as geographical meanings attached to the distinctions. As the various linguistic atlases produced in recent years prove, geographically localized dialects are thought to subsist almost wholly in small rural communities, the urbanized non-standard speech being regarded as less 'pure' dialect.

Some American linguists have pointed out that the European assumption that 'cultivated' speech is uniform does not apply to the USA.[72] Historically, the great American cities such as Boston, Charleston, Cincinnati, Nashville and San Francisco, served as the cultural centres of vast settlements. Consequently, it has been argued that American standard speech as well as American folk speech has local variants. It would seem, however, that these linguists have phonological criteria in mind rather than grammatical. American children do not learn different grammars in different states. Their habitual choices of grammatical options will, of course, in some ways reflect their immediate linguistic environment. Lexically, there are distinctions which may rightly be attributed to dialectal differences, even in the dialect we call Standard English. But, as we shall see, the greatest single characteristic of American English is its uniformity.

A conspicuous example of apparently social distinctions within SE is to be found in the work of A. S. C. Ross, Nancy Mitford and others in describing U and non-U English in England.[73] Apart from phonological distinctions, it was suggested, upper-class speech was characterized by lexical preferences such as *lavatory* instead of the non-U *toilet, dinner-napkin* instead of *serviette* and so on. Ross's original essays attempted to show how the speaker with middle- or lower-class upbringing could betray his social origins in his speech by such 'genteelisms' as the non-U *mirror* for the U *looking-glass, domestic* for *servant, lounge* for *sitting-room* and *couch* for *sofa*. Many of the so-called markers of U vocabulary, however, are to be found in the idiolects of socially humble people brought up in rural areas, where they suggest traditional schooling and slowness of change more than anything else, and the mass media and universal education have to a large extent ironed out such differences as existed. No doubt there are still enclaves of 'upper-class' English here and there, but their speech cannot be called superior in any significant way, either linguistically or socially. It is difficult to persuade people, however, that a socially prestigious way of speaking is not necessarily a *superior* way of speaking.

It has been seen (p. 32) that there is a well-established relationship between social background and educational attainment, and that many authorities have associated educational disadvantage with some linguistic deficiency. It has been argued that the dialect learned by lower-class children creates educational problems because it is an inferior vehicle for the reception and production of complex utterances. This 'language deficit' theory has resulted in many compensatory programmes designed to give children and their parents greater linguistic versatility. If their native dialect is educationally less useful, the idea was, give them access to SE. A more 'progressive' solution was that the native dialect should not be 'replaced' by SE but that SE should be added to their repertoire. But the 'deficit hypothesis' has now been largely discredited. Linguists such as Labov, Macaulay and Trudgill have shown that there is nothing *linguistically* inferior about the dialects of lower-class people: they are quite capable of expressing the deepest possible thoughts, the subtlest possible logical distinctions, the sweetest of emotions. Any dialect of English is potentially just as powerful a vehicle of communication as any other dialect. The apparent educational disadvantage derives from *social*, not linguistic, causes.[74]

It is quite evident, of course, that the child who can understand and speak *only* a dialect different from the SE used in school will be at a disadvantage. In learning to read, for example, he has a double task to perform: firstly to learn to understand spoken SE and secondly to learn to read written SE. With this in mind some educators conceived the idea of teaching dialect-speaking children to read texts specially printed in their own dialect.[75] Although this has not proved effective there can be little doubt that the teacher who can operate in the children's own dialect will prove more successful than the teacher whose working dialect is alien to his pupils. Labov, Macaulay and others have shown, however, that it is the attitudes of people that really matter: lower-class dialect speakers have low self-concepts which they associate with their own speechways.

The intrinsic linguistic integrity of non-standard dialects can be demonstrated. It can be shown, for example, that the grammar of the dialect is internally consistent, so that although *I seen him* is deviant from SE it is not an 'error' *within* the dialect itself. It can be shown that so far as grammar is concerned there can be no appeal to the superior logicality or consistency of standard forms. For example, the use of double or multiple negatives which characterizes some non-standard dialects is quite common in the standard versions of many languages, and was an integral feature of the temporal dialect of English used in Shakespeare's time. Even today the non-standard *I didn't never hit nobody* has its parallel in the upper-class idiom *I shouldn't wonder if it didn't rain*. Another example that could be cited is the use, in some non-standard dialects, of a plural form of *you* (*youse*). This shows a consistency not found in SE, which uses plural forms for all the other personal pronouns but not *you*.[76]

It is very difficult, however, to make accurate observations about any one dialect, social or geographical, for the simple reason that it is virtually impossible to identify a given dialect. In any English-speaking country there is a 'dialect continuum', both geographically and socially. That is to say, dialects gradually merge into one another as one travels east to west or north to south,[77] and in any one community (if you can demarcate a community) there will be 'layers' of dialect as one's attention moves 'down' the social scale from SE, which one may assume persists as the universal 'top' social dialect. As one distinguished dialectologist puts it:

> There may exist in any given community a complex linguistic situation, for members of the community may differ greatly, both in pronunciation and other non-phonetic matters, in the way they talk. At one end of the scale there is, in many places, the 'broad' local dialect speaker who is least affected by any influence from outside; at the other there may be someone whose speech has no regional characteristics at all. In between these extremes, there may be many intermediate types of speech, and some people will have more than one at their command, each available for appropriate occasions.[78]

Geographical dialects of English display an astonishing variety and richness of invention. The half-million or so words which comprise the lexicon printed in a 'non-abridged' dictionary is but the visible part of the lexical iceberg that is English. Dictionaries of dialects contain a fascinating collection of local words, some of them survivals from a distant past and some recent coinages. People make their own language.

American English

As already observed (p. 118), the most important single characteristic of American English (AE) is its uniformity. Despite many differences in accent throughout the USA, American English is remarkably homogeneous. This can be explained by the history of settlement which began in 1607 and still continues.[79] New England was settled by people who came mainly from the southern half of England, two-thirds of them (about 16,000 by 1640) from the eastern counties. New York contained a small community of Dutch people before it was taken over by the English in 1664; a century later it was wholly dominated by English settlers from Connecticut. Pennsylvania was settled in the latter decades of the seventeenth century by English Quakers, Scotch-Irish, Welsh and some Germans. In the middle of the eighteenth century it was settled by nearly 50,000 Scotch-Irish – people whose ancestors were Scottish but who had been 'planted' in Ulster by Cromwell. The South Atlantic settlements of Virginia and the Carolinas were made by people from all parts of Britain. The Middle West was settled by a mixture of people from all of the thirteen original colonies. The Far West was settled by people from the mid-west, the east and the south. Thus the general pattern of settlement was that each new area was populated by people from other areas. There was a constant intermingling of people, largely of British stock: the French, German and Dutch settlers were too sparse in numbers to avoid being assimilated. The linguistic diversity of Britain resulted from the isolation of communities in geographical pockets. The linguistic uniformity of the United States is the result of quite opposite circumstances.

The geographical vastness of America has been matched by the adventurous mobility of its people. The standardizing effect of this on American English was noticed quite early in its history, and some writers, such as Witherspoon and Fenimore Cooper, were inspired to believe that Americans could develop an English that was superior to British English by its 'purity' and 'accuracy' – both terms meaning the *consistency* resulting from the absence of local variation. It would appear that two psychological influences make for the standardization of a language. The first is the tendency for a speaker entering a new community to try to suppress as far as he can the deviant features of his speech, so as not to be ridiculed. The second is the natural desire of a speaker to acquire the speech characteristics of the majority in order to be accepted socially and to identify himself with the dominant elements in the community. For these reasons, as well as the pattern of settlement, there is a strong tendency towards homogeneity in the speech of immigrants. As we shall see, the same characteristic is true of Australian English.

Another factor making for linguistic homogeneity in America was the consciousness of a new national identity which inspired many cultural leaders to plead for the means to establish a new American version of the English language. Noah Webster was the most notable of many American scholars who urged the promulgation of new standards in grammar, lexis and spelling which would justify the notion of an American language independent of British English comparisons. Early in their history Americans began to propose the establishment of academic research and controlling institutions to promote the efficient use of language. In the event, however, they have relied, like the British, on the punditry of lexicographers and grammarians rather than on a formal Academy on the French model. But American interest in American English has remained strong, and the linguistic nationalism of Webster has survived vigorously. Even today there are many who prefer to call their language *American* rather than *English*.

The American English that developed through the crowded history of the eighteenth and nineteenth centuries was lexically enriched by various cultural forces.[80] It acquired many Amerindian words such as *hickory, hooch, kayak, moose, squaw, totem*; some French words such as *apache, brave* (the noun), *bureau, levee, cache, chowder* (from *chaudière*), *prairie, pumpkin, rapids*; some Spanish words such as *bonanza, bronco, cockroach, creole, lasso, patio, ranch, stampede, vigilante*; and some Dutch words such as *bedspread, boss, dumb* (meaning stupid), *cookie, dope, sleigh, stoop*; some German words such as *noodle, pretzel, sauerkraut*. The early colonists invented new words to describe the new natural environment that confronted them: *bluff, foothill, gap, divide, watershed, clearing*. They adapted familiar English words and combined them to form new items such as *sidewalk, lightning rod, spelling bee, low-down, know-nothing, wire-pulling, sitting on the fence, war-path, paleface, scalp, bullfrog*. Wave after wave of immigrants from Europe added their contributions to the lexicon through the nineteenth century: words from Italian (*pizza, spaghetti, minestrone*), German (*delicatessen, hamburger, poker, seminar, semester*), Hungarian (*goulash*), Spanish (*vanilla, alligator, mosquito*). The vigorous American politicians coined new terms to connote new institutions: *assemblyman, bandwagon, caucus, congressional, presidential, filibuster*.

Differences between present-day Standard American English (SAE) and Standard English English (SEE) may be seen in grammar, lexis and pronunciation. (Spelling differences were described in Chapter 3.) There are some points to be made, however, before these differences are discussed. In the first place, the differences are minute and insignificant in comparison to the similarities, which are such that it is not possible to regard SAE and SEE as different *languages*; they are different *Englishes*. Secondly, a number of differences may be observed between SAE and SEE which are similar to differences observable between SEE and other British versions of the language, notably Standard Scots English (SSE). Thirdly, the English-speaking areas of the world today are in continuous intensive contact through the mass media, so it is scarcely possible to identify any one instance of difference which may not be in process of being cross-culturally absorbed. The following observations, therefore, are gross generalizations.

In pronunciation there are some differences resulting from the fact that AE developed from a temporal dialect of English transported with the settlers in the seventeenth century. For this reason it has often been asserted that American pronunciation is probably more like Shakespeare's than is RP. SAE has preserved the sound of *r* before vowels and consonants and at word-endings, whereas in RP the *r* sound occurs only before a vowel. Thus in such words as *car, bare, more, cure, turf* and many more SAE has the *r* sound and RP has no *r* sound. (SSE also retains the *r* sound in such words, as do Irish, Welsh, Cornish and other varieties of SE. RP is, in this and other respects, the minority system.) SAE has also preserved a flat *a* sound, as in *path, fast, laugh* (where the vowel is the *a* sound of *pan*); since the early nineteenth century RP has used a broad *a* in such words. Again, SAE speakers pronounce *either* and *neither* with a long *e* (as in *teeth*) while in RP the sound has been diphthongized.

Some features of the grammar of SAE have also descended from the speech of the early colonists. A widely quoted example is the SAE *gotten* contrasting with the SEE *got*. *You could have gotten what you wanted* would be recognized at once as an American construction by English people. Even in Scotland, where *gotten* is common in local dialect or colloquial speech, *got* is the SSE form. Many Americans would still say *dove* (*dived*) and *clumb* (*climbed*) though these are now looked on as substandard. Like the Scots, Americans tend to say 'She's in the hospital' where English speakers omit the article. Americans and Scots will also say 'all of the time', 'all of the papers' where the SEE has 'all the . . .'[81]

American vocabulary retains some connotations now lost in SEE though some are returning via American influences: *fall* for autumn, *rare* meat, *platter, I guess, I reckon*. But it is much more characteristic of Americans that they so readily innovate in language. They have invented many verbs from nouns: *to radio, to chair a meeting, to materialize, attitudinize*, and so on. They have coined nouns from verbs: *brush off, input, check-up*. They invented names for their inventions: *telephone, cablegram, telegram, automobile*.

In many ways, the lexicon of SAE differs from that of any other English simply because Americans named things for themselves as they introduced them. It is interesting, for example, that British *railway* people drew upon old coaching terms – *drivers, coaches, guards, booking office* – while American *railroad* men use *cars, engineers, conductors, ticket offices*. Similarly the British *lift* and *tram* are *elevator* and *electric car* in the USA. SEE has *trousers, braces, waistcoat* while SAE has *pants, suspenders, vest*. A British motor car has a *boot*, a *bonnet* and *bumpers*, where the American automobile has a *trunk*, a *hood* and *fenders*. The vocabularies differ because they emerged from and reflect different cultures.

American English has been influenced in a subtle way by the speech habits of immigrants whose mother tongue was not English. For example, as Fritz Spiegl has pointed out,[82] the colloquial expression 'No way' which has recently become fashionable is probably a translation of the German *keineswegs*. When Americans use the conditional 'In the event that . . .' they are echoing a German phrase. The expression 'Have a coffee' (as against 'Have tea' or 'Have some tea') suggests the German *einen Kaffee*. The American readiness to use *wise* as a suffix echoes the German use of *weise*. The use of an unrelated adverb at the beginning of a sentence – 'Hopefully, it won't happen', 'Predictably, the house fell down' – is a German convention.

Like every English-speaking country, the United States contains many dialect-using communities. In the main the dialects are characterized by deviations from SAE which are not educationally significant: that is, the young dialect speaker will have little or no difficulty in coping with the SE demands of schooling. In some areas the dialect is regarded with considerable relish as a heritage from an earlier age. The 'Mountain English' of Kentucky, for example, is enjoyed by visitors as a 'quaint or picturesque' representation of the 'old English', a hillbilly being defined as 'somebody who lives in the hill country and speaks the language of Shakespeare'.[83] Some of the expressions are certainly relics of the past: *a-fixin' to* (getting ready to), *airish* (breezy), *layin' off* (postponing), *plumb* (completely), *sallit greens* (spring salad plants), *smack dab* (point-blank). But a so-called dictionary of Mountain English contains many more jokey items mocking the pronunciation: *canechair* (can't hear); *chore* (possessive pronoun, e.g. 'Is that chore dog?'); *faints* (fence); *far place* (fireplace); *Oh high* (Ohio). Like the famous Southern drawl, regional dialects of this kind reflect a linguistic diversity which underlies the apparent homogeneity of American English, but which (setting aside a small proportion of the lexis) is almost wholly a matter of accent, rhythm and pronunciation.

The speech of Black Americans, on the other hand, constitutes an important dialect of American English. Black American English (BAE) resulted from the interaction of the West African slaves and the white men who exploited them. It is still debatable whether or not BAE is a creolized form of English. Where English-speakers have made prolonged contact with people of inferior status as in the West and East Indies, they have together developed a pidgin English, which is grammatically and lexically simplified. When a pidgin becomes the main language of a people, with a greatly re-expanded vocabulary and a developed grammar, it is known as a creolized language. BAE is not a pidgin, but it may be a creolized form of English resulting from an earlier pidgin. On the other hand, some linguists argue that BAE is the actual dialect of Southern poor whites with various accretions from African languages. Whatever the scientific truth of the matter, it has been amply demonstrated that BAE has its own phonological, grammatical and lexical structures.[84]

These distinctive characteristics make BAE educationally significant in that its speakers are confronted with certain new linguistic demands when they enter formal schooling. Whether or not the differences between BAE and SAE are themselves important factors in causing difficulty for black students has not yet been fully resolved, since BAE is spoken by socio-economically depressed people. As we have seen, there can be nothing *linguistically* inferior in BAE. Obviously, however, you will be *educationally* disadvantaged if you are not at ease with the dialect in which your teacher operates. Efficient schooling must devise the means to overcome this disadvantage, by increasing the linguistic versatility of the child and by acknowledging the cultural integrity of his dialect.

Australian English

Australian Standard English exhibits no significant grammatical differences from SE as it is spoken and written elsewhere. The distinctive peculiarities of Australian SE lie in its pronunciation and vocabulary. Even in these respects, however, only a very small proportion of Australian spoken SE varies significantly, and even less of its written SE.[85] It is true that an Australian accent is easily recognizable, especially in America, mainly because of a tendency to use very broad allophones of certain phonemes. The Australian saying *lake* or *day*, for example, might be misheard as saying *like* or *die* — but only by someone unaccustomed to the Australian voice. A feature of the Australian manner of speaking which has often been mentioned is the drawl: that is, a tendency to speak in a slow and rhythmically even way. But it is probable that this is more of a general impression than a demonstrable fact.[86]

Australian English, like American English, is remarkably homogeneous, there being few regional variations. This is usually ascribed to the 'mixing bowl theory': the settlers came from different dialectal areas of Britain and consciously standardized their speechways so as to make social cohesion more effective. The great majority of early Australian settlers came from London. Their speech was urban, working-class; many were convicts who, though not necessarily criminal, naturally employed a prisoners' argot. By the 1830s a distinct Australian English was emerging, and the subsequent waves of Irish, Scottish and Welsh immigrants contributed little more than some dialect vocabulary to the language. As in America, so in Australia the seminal settlements tended to be created by colonists from another part of the country rather than new immigrants, and the standardizing tendency was strengthened through the social mobility of the people.

Like the early American settlers, the Australian colonists needed new terms to describe the unfamiliar features of landscape, flora and fauna in their new home. They employed the age-old techniques of extending, adapting and compounding old words. Words like *brush, creek, scrub, lagoon, gully* were introduced to aid travelling and surveying. Strange trees were given familiar names (*apple-tree, native pear, oak*) or were named by sawyers with new compounds (*beefwood, ironbark, lightwood*) or were given the Aboriginal names (*quandong, mulga, brigalow, kurrajong*). Aboriginal names were borrowed to denote birds and animals: *budgerigar, koala, dingo, wallaby, wombat*. (Curiously enough, the word *kangaroo*, brought to Europe by Captain Cook, entered English and French before Australia was colonized.)

Aboriginal names were naturally employed for Aboriginal weapons and customs: *woomera, boomerang, corroboree, jumbuck*.

Australians made extensive use of compounds, this being always the ordinary person's favourite way of neologizing. The most common roots used were *bush* (*bushfire, bush-horse, bush-hut, bushman* – and later *bush telegraph, bush-lawyer, bush-walk, bushwhacker*); *stock* (*stock-farm, stock-holder, stock-house, stock-run*); *station* (*cattle station, sheep station, stock station, head station*).

The British civil servants and colonial administrators who managed the settlement of Australia employed the same methods as were used for the settling and management of the American colonies, so they used the same terminology. Hence we have words like *block, location, section, township* in common between the two Englishes. *Bushranger*, now firmly associated with Australia, was one of these words. In much the same way, military terms came to be used by Australian farmers: *muster, overseer*. In the mid-nineteenth-century gold rushes, mining terms such as *stuff, tailings* were introduced. The Scottish farmers who settled the New England district introduced terms from sheep and cattle husbandry: *bail, paddock, snig*.

In the twentieth century Australian English has contributed a number of colloquialisms to British English: to feel *crook, starve the crows, bust a gut, put in the boot, get stuck into*, to get a *fair crack of the whip*. Despite this, however, Australian English has always accreted more from other Englishes than it has dispensed. Like all the other varieties of English, it has acquired many Americanisms since the onset of the talking film in the 1930s. Because of the close cultural and socio-economic affinities of the two nations, British English has exerted a strong influence on Australian English even in modern times. But there can be no denying the fact that, though they speak the English of the world more certainly than almost any other English-speaking people, Australians have their own distinctive variety of the language, which is theirs alone and is continuously becoming what some scholars would prefer to call *Austral* rather than *English*.

English in New Zealand

The New Zealand accent, like that of Australians, has a strong superficial resemblance to that of the London Cockney, mainly because of the broad allophones of the phonemes in such words as *made, lake, major*. The phoneme in such words as *art, large, master*, on the other hand, is given the flatter sound characteristic of American New Englanders.[87] The influence of the large element of Scots settlers is displayed by the pronunciation of *wh-* words as if they spelled *hw-* and (in the Otago district particularly) of the rolled *r*. In general, however, the pronunciation habits of New Zealanders are similar to those of Australians.

The pastoral economy of the early settlers explains the presence in New Zealand English (NZE) of such words as *bush*, with its compounds *bush-hawk, bushwarbler, bush wren, bush sickness*, etc. The NZE equivalent of *sharefarmer* and *sharecropper* is *sharemilker*. *Paddock* and *byre* recall the original Scots settlers. *Section, line, back-blocks* and similar words shared with America and Australia recall the terminology of the British colonial administrators and surveyors. The vocabulary of dairy farmers, timber workers, paper manufacturers, woolstores and other occupations retain many words originating from similar occupations in Britain.

Since New Zealand has developed its own institutions – its educational system, for instance – it is natural that these should have their own terminologies. G. W. Turner mentions that New Zealanders colloquially refer to university as *varsity* while Australians say *uni*; that New Zealand children have a *shelter shed* in the playground while some Australians have a *lunch shed* or *weather shed*, and have a morning *playtime* instead of the Australian *recess*. Although many New Zealand terms are familiar to British (especially Scottish) ears, they are sufficiently distinctive to warrant being labelled NZE.

In his essay on NZE written in 1943, J. A. W. Bennett mentions some Maori words adopted into NZE. These included *pakeha* (white men), *kai* (food), *kit* (basket), *kiwi* (a flightless bird), *taipo* (devil), *hoot* (money), *tapu* (taboo), *pukkaroo* (worthless). Twenty years later G. W. Turner states that the Maori language no longer contributes greatly to NZE vocabulary. He mentions *Maoritonga* (Maori ways and culture), *marae* (referring to the oratory and community organization of the Maori meeting house), and *pakeha* which is now extending its meaning to take on political connotations. A remarkable feature of linguistics in New Zealand is the respect now being paid to the Maori language and culture. Correct Maori pronunciation of place names on television, and the teaching of Maori to student teachers are both healthy signs of social progress. In educational terms there can be no doubt that this will promote linguistic sensitivity and competence in the children of both social stocks.

English as a *lingua franca*: West Indian, African, Indian

The West Indies

The Negro English of the West Indies displaced various African dialects spoken by the earliest generations of slaves. The creolized language resulting from the succeeding generations' closer association with the English of the British has its own phonological and grammatical structures, and it is nowadays subject to much research.[88] There are different varieties in different islands, and there is a discernible 'scale' of variation between the SE of the British expatriates at one end, the localized creole at the other and, in the important position of being the true standard form, West Indian Standard English (WIS). The vocabulary and grammar of WIS is largely the same as those of SE, the major differences being in pronunciation. F. G. Cassidy wrote in 1961 that the educated Jamaican pronounced English as well as any other educated speaker and with a distinctive pattern of intonation: his speech is more accented than that of the Englishman or American, going up and down more frequently, and by sharper rises and falls: 'it has a decided and characteristic lilt'.[89] According to Kenneth Ramchand, speakers of WIS can be recognized by the fact that, although they can control the grammar and lexis of SE, because they are more or less instinctive speakers of or thinkers in a native West Indian dialect they retain the WIS pronunciation habits. The ability to speak a West Indian dialect will, of course, allow the WIS speaker to lapse consciously or not into dialect grammatical habits, such as the tendency to do without tense markers.

South Africa

In South Africa English coexists with Afrikaans, a creole resulting, it has been suggested, from a pidgin used for communication between Dutch settlers and Africans. The English-speaking South Africans speak SE, without regional variations. Their pronunciation is similar to that of SEE but with some Afrikaans influences: for example, the narrowing of the vowel in such words as *cab* (pronounced *keb*) and *pen* (pronounced *pin*). South Africans share with Scots and Americans the tendency to voice *r* when it appears in the spelling. Like Scots, Americans and New Zealanders, too, they tend to distribute stress evenly over a sequence of syllables, so that they will not slur over a word like *extraordinary* as the English do.[90]

South African English acquired some Afrikaans vocabulary which has entered world English: *commando, commandeer, trek, apartheid, veldt*. It has retained a number of words which are distinctively South African: *braaiveleis* (a barbecue), *donga* (ravine), *kopje* (hill), *mealies* (maize). Like the English of other former colonies, South African English has retained some terms, such as *location, camp, land* used by early administrators and surveyors. It has preserved some words which are familiar to Americans: *store, storekeeper, cookies, up-country, divide* (watershed). In the main, however, the English of the white South African differs little from the SE spoken throughout the world.

The English of the educated black and coloured South African is hardly distinguishable from that of the whites, but the lower class social dialects of English spoken by blacks exhibits features of mother tongue interference. According to L. W. Lanham, few Africans in the republic now acquire English by assimilation; almost all black children have their first real contact with English at school, taught by black teachers who themselves do not have a firm control of standard English. In an essay published in 1965 Lanham argued that unless there was a massive increase in the use of modern technology and improved teaching techniques the English of black South Africans would drastically deteriorate.[91]

African states

Mother tongue interference is, of course, a feature of the English spoken by all students whose first language is not English. In some parts of Africa this constitutes such a problem that it can be difficult for people in one African country to understand the English spoken by people from another African country. But all of the African states which have adopted English as the official language (or an official co-language) for law, commerce, education and so on are fully aware of this problem. African nations spend up to half their annual budgets on education, and a high proportion of this goes towards the teaching of English. In Kenya, Ghana, Nigeria, Sierra Leone and Zambia, English is the principal language; in Malawi it coexists as a principal language with Nyanja; in Tanzania it coexists with Swahili. It would be wrong to say that English is a foreign language in those countries, and yet it is a second language for the vast majority of the inhabitants.

English is an extremely useful language in these African countries. Where tribal languages abound, and are continual threats to national unity, English constitutes an acceptable *lingua franca*. It is all the more acceptable because it is already, for historical reasons, an international language. Although it is still widely associated with the British colonial domination, the repugnance that would naturally flow from that is largely offset by the consciousness that it is also the language of America. Again, English is known to have originated from a number of separate languages, and to have accumulated vocabulary from all corners of the world. Its international use as a *lingua franca* makes its internal use the more palatable. Finally, because it is so widely spoken in the world, English is the most economical language by which to gain access to knowledge. No other language produces so many books as does English, and because of its world-wide incidence, English is more frequently taught as a second language than any other.

No doubt the varieties of English spoken in the English-speaking African countries differ from one another in various ways, but too little scholarship is freely available to allow for general comparisons. As detailed descriptions of SE as spoken in, for example, Nigeria or Kenya become available it will be possible to perceive trends. In the meantime there is a growing volume of major literature written by Africans: the work of Achebe, Okara and others exhibits the potential of a West African Standard English. Gabriel Okara, in his novel, *The Voice* (Heinemann, 1970), illustrates a conscious use of constructions from his native Ijaw brought into the syntax of English:

> It was the day's ending and Okalo by a window stood. Okalo stood looking at the sun behind the tree tops falling. The river was flowing, reflecting the finishing sun, like a dying away memory.

India

Of all the former British-dominated countries, India has the longest experience of English as a dominant second language. The number of borrowings into English from Indian and Dravidian dialects testifies to the long history of association: *pundit* (from Hindu, first used in English in 1672), *bungalow* (from Hindu, 1676), *bandana* (1752), *cheetah* (1781), *shampoo* (1762), *sari* (1785), *bangle* (1787), *thug* (1810), *pyjamas* (1886); *calico* (from Dravidian, 1540), *coolie* (1598), *curry* (1598), *atoll* (1625), *teak* (1698).

For the educated Indian, even one whose mother tongue is an Indian language, English is not a foreign language. It is a language he will have been familiar with from childhood. It is the language in which he may have learned to read; certainly it would be the language in which he learned mathematics and other intellectual disciplines. Indian English has its own characteristic pronunciation system, its own features of grammar and lexis. Standard Indian English (SIE) has a whole vocabulary of greetings, blessings and curses which are indigenous. In general, however, SIE differs from SEE only in its phonology, and these distinctive features are seldom of much significance, the major variations from RP being the use of retroflection in pronouncing *t, d, n, l** and, in some areas, the intrusion of an initial vocalic sound in words beginning with *st, sp* and *sk*.

Conclusion

In this chapter I have offered brief descriptions of some varieties of Standard English, each of which is dominant in its own way. There is, however, a World Standard English, and I have set out to demonstrate this by showing that the Englishes standardized in various countries are all manifestations of the same language. In each country, however, there are non-standard dialects of English, and it is important to understand the difference between Standard English and its non-standard relations. In the next Chapter I deal with questions of good and bad English, 'correctness' and 'appropriateness', and what is really meant by 'standards'.

* Retroflex consonants are produced with the tip of the tongue curled back.

CHAPTER 6

The Uses of English

Introduction

What *is* good English? If you have read this far in the book, and have
been able to accept the information and inferences I have presented,
you will agree that this is a very difficult, complex question. English is
not one whole language: it is an assemblage of varieties of language.
There is English English, Scots English, American English, Australian
English ... and there are Standard English and non-Standard
English dialects in every English-speaking country. To make matters
more complicated, this chapter deals with the ways in which the
speaker of English uses different selections of the language
in different situations for different purposes. At the end of this
final chapter, I hope that the answer to the question will be quite
apparent and explicit: *good English is English that does the job you want it
to do.*

English and Situation[92]

Dialects are varieties of the language resulting from *where you live* and
how you live. Another set of language varieties are *diatypes*, which result
from *where* and *when* and *why* you use language: in other words, from
the situation in which the language is used. Diatypes of English can
be identified by characteristics of the *field of discourse,* the *mode of discourse* and the *tenor of discourse.* The selection of the grammar, lexis
and semantics employed in a given situation – that is, the *register*
being used – results from elements of these three features of
discourse.

A major influence on our choice of language – of the syntax and
vocabulary we decide to wrap the linguistic message in – is the *field of
discourse.* The field of discourse is the 'subject' of communication,
what the language is about, what is going on when you are communicating. Perhaps the most common of all fields of discourse is
phatic communion,[93] the social 'chat' we indulge in for the purpose of
making and maintaining personal contact with others. As Hayakawa

said in his important book, *Language in Thought and Action*, 'the prevention of silence is itself an important function of speech'.[94] We select this field in ordinary social intercourse, orally or in informal personal letters. The topics we pursue in phatic communion are usually greetings, observations about the weather, the immediate environment, some recent national event, and so on – the petty currency of social life. In certain communities you will hear of favourite topics: in England and Australia, among men, cricket; in New York, among men, the World Series; everywhere, among women, prices. The language used in phatic communion tends to be simple, short sentences, informal, cheerful or ruefully woebegone. In the course of a day we participate in different episodes with different people: with the family; then, later, with fellow travellers; then with colleagues, and so on.

The field of discourse which gossip or idle chatter or 'passing the time of day' inhabit is a non-technical one. Most fields of discourse are technical fields, where the English used has certain special features. The subject matter is known to the participants, so that technical terms with specialized meanings can be used without explanation. The vocabulary used to contextualize the technical terms also tends to be specialized: this means that certain words, which are not themselves technical, tend to accompany, or encapsulate, the technical terms. For example, the field of discourse of this book, which can be generally labelled *linguistics*, requires many technical terms which you have already encountered: *semantic, discourse, rhetoric, clause, variety* and so on. But these technical terms are usually accompanied by specialized uses of quite ordinary words such as *develop, rules, applies, operating, store, predict* and so on. These are words which *collocate*, or keep company with, the technical terminology of the specialist field.

Certain favourite grammatical patterns also recur in a particular field of discourse. For example, some kinds of discourse will employ many long noun phrases – such as *the fifth left intercostal space* in anatomy or *an orange-coloured precipitate of antimony sulphide, Sb_2S_3* in chemistry – which you take in your stride if you know the field. In some fields, passive verb phrases recur: this is characteristic of discourse in the physical sciences. The *religion* field of discourse, in sermons and prayers, is characterized by vocative elements ('O Almighty and most merciful God . . .'), the use of the otherwise archaic *thou*, and long sentences with many parenthetical elements.

Creative writers can sometimes capture the features of a particular field of discourse with a few typical words. John Betjeman thus delineates the 'Executive':

You ask me what it is I do.
Well actually, you know,
I'm partly a liaison man and partly PRO.
Essentially I integrate the current export drive
And basically I'm viable from ten o'clock till five.[95]

And a field of discourse can be characterized by what could be described as 'specialized clichés'. Here is a *Guardian* leader-writer on 'trade union parlance':

Clichés in cuckooland

In trade union parlance cloud cuckoo land is the intellectual territory occupied by a person whose wishes or intentions are so patently unrealistic as to make them fit objects of ridicule and contempt. Thus Mr Sidney Weighell of the railwaymen's union was said by a spokesman of some of his members to be living in cloud cuckoo land when he proposed cuts in overtime and the recruitment of more staff, for it is generally agreed that such a method of reducing unemployment and increasing the efficiency of the railways cannot be worth serious examination. The vicarage tea party, again in trade union parlance, is a state of affairs the tranquillity of which is invoked to illustrate the magnitude of an impending or hypothetical upheaval, as for instance when a negotiator might say: If the bosses think they can stick to a derisory $22\frac{1}{2}$ per cent the lads will make the Second World War look like a vicarage tea party. The teddy-bears' picnic is a local variant of the same essentially pacific occurrence, and it is interesting that popular usage should be so many years behind events as to place vicars and teddy-bears in the same category. The vicars of this trade union imagery are gentle, self-effacing persons like Mr Harding, the precentor of Trollope's Barchester, whereas today, as the Dean of Peterhouse demonstrated in this week's *Sunday Telegraph*, the entire clergy of the Church of England is a rabble, not knowing what it is supposed to be doing and latching on to the latest social fashion as a godsend. But perhaps we digress. Indeed, there is no perhaps about it: we do digress.

The point is that apart from the opening and closing prices industrial negotiations could, if desired, be conducted almost entirely from a trade union glossary of figures of speech in which both cloud cuckoo land and the vicarage tea party would find a place. It is a world in which chickens are hatched and then come home to roost, in which mountains are made out of molehills and horses swapped in midstream, in which nettles are grasped and bulls taken by horns. Not all the similes are rustic, for when there is money on the table it often follows that there is light at the end of the tunnel, and when men make beds they must lie on them. In more constructive negotiations bridges are not crossed before they are reached, though some bridges are known to have been played by ear. It may be that Britain will always escape out-and-out class war because the language is not suited to it. People who are batting on sticky wickets or out making hay while the sun shines cannot, as on the Continent, be strung up from the nearest lamp-post.[96]

Vocabulary which appears to be specialist but which is in reality unnecessary because it is not needed to convey special meanings is known as *jargon*. Policemen are traditionally charged with using jargon, as are civil servants. Jargon is associated with the use of such words as *situation* ('He was seen lying in a recumbent situation'), the use of the suffix *-wise* ('Architecture-wise the situation was promising'), and the vague use of words such as *structure, infrastructure, meaningful* and *basis* which have a spurious air of scientific objectivity. In another sense, jargon may be language which in itself may be used legitimately for 'internal' communication among people with specialist knowledge but which is incomprehensible to those who do not have that knowledge. Thus the language of the legal document may be labelled jargon, although, to lawyers, it is clearly useful and economical. Some fields of discourse require English which must be learned by the users: for example, gardening, knitting, automobile engineering, chess. Once learned, the language is economical and lucid; that, of course, is its purpose.

Language varies also in accordance with the *modes of discourse*. The most obvious distinction between modes of discourse is that between the speech mode and the writing mode. As we have seen (in Chapter 3), there are important differences between spoken and written English. The language we use – the choice we make of syntactic patterns and of vocabulary – will vary in accordance with whether we are communicating in speech or in writing. In speech, however, we must distinguish between different situations: our language will vary according to whether we speak casually, without rehearsal, or with more deliberation (say, when taking part in a serious discussion), or when lecturing, which is an activity akin to uttering written-English aloud. Certain markers of casual or spontaneous interchange, such as the use of *hesitation phenomena* like 'm-m' and 'er', are absent from the more deliberate speech of the lecturer. Other features of conversation are *silence fillers,* such as 'sort of', 'you know', 'I mean', and *intimacy signals* such as 'you know me' and 'as you know'. It is possible, however, to speak 'at' another person or group in an apparently casual way but, in actuality, to be monopolizing the situation. *Monologuing* is one type of controlled discourse: the speaker (a teacher in the classroom, for instance, or a lawyer in court) does not expect to be interrupted and yet is making eye-to-eye contact with his audience. Many a teacher monologues in this way, assuming that his pupils are listening and so learning. In fact, the pupils may be doing little more than facing him – 'pupilling', this has been called. Monologue speech is more coherent than casual conversation. Monologuing is a skill acquired by people whose occupation requires it: sports commentators, teachers, journalists. Between spontaneous speech and the written text comes the mode of discourse called non-spontaneous speech. This may be the recitation of a prepared (but not necessarily written) text. Early civilizations had 'oral literatures' with rhetors famed for reciting epics and speeches. Or it may be reading aloud a text written for this purpose: a lecture, a dialogue, a poem or sermon.

The other general mode of discourse, written English, is also sub-divisible into different categories. There is the *disjunctive mode*,[97] which carries simple, usually short messages: examples are public notices, catalogue entries, addresses on envelopes, titles of books. The *abbreviated mode* (such as is used for headlines and telegrams), like the disjunctive mode, has its own grammar and style of presentation. For example, the abbreviated mode employs a special kind of non-finite predicator. In the following headlines the 'Pn' is the non-finite predicator, the S is the subject, the C the complement and the A the adjunct:

S / Pn / A
Council / to vote / tomorrow.

S / Pn
Mr Smith's Cabinet / resigns.

A / S / Pn / C
Now / Army / counts / cost.

The literary mode of discourse is divisible into *genres* such as epic, sonnet, novel, short story, dramatic monologue, and so on. Each genre has its own conventions of presentation, its own stylistic preferences. In narrative fiction, the dialogue is written language meant to be read, not spoken: yet it is meant to represent speech. In some novels, such as James Joyce's *Ulysses*, different genres are represented within the whole work. *Ulysses* includes the 'interior monologue', which is supposed to represent the thoughts of a character as they run through her mind: this can be described as language written to be 'thought' along with the character.

Tenors of discourse are another class of language varieties which must be identified if we are to understand how we match our English to the situation in which we are using it. The tenor of discourse is the result of the relationship that exists between the users of language in a situation. Tenor can express the degree of formality that exists between people, and changes in the status of the relationship will be reflected in the language they use with one another. Total strangers meeting for the first time will certainly not use the kind of language that intimate friends use: for example, the expressions that signal intimacy ('old boy', 'good buddy', 'honey'). In some communities, people will not address each other by their first names until they are friendly; in other social groups first names come easily. In some groups of colleagues in England the last name is used as a sign of professional comradeship, but this is regarded as 'cold' and 'stand-offish' in Scotland and would even be insulting in certain parts of the English-speaking world. Often, the use of a first name is taken to signal the desire to be more friendly; but it is well known that there is an immensely complex protocol surrounding the addressor-addressee relationship in professional circles. This is only one of the more easily perceived aspects of the linguistic expression of interpersonal relationships. In fact every aspect of a speech act will change as the status of a relationship changes – the intonation patterns, the syntax and the lexis. Even the quantity of language will vary with the degree of formality. An intimately acquainted couple will normally require less language to fulfil their communicative needs than people who are less familiar with one another.

Functional tenor has to do with the purposes and intentions of the language user: what the language is being used *for* — to persuade, threaten, encourage, ingratiate oneself, and so on. Your purpose will lead you to select certain grammatical and lexical and phonological items rather than others.

Some varieties of language are called *registers*. These are varieties of English which exhibit features resulting from the social context in which the language is used. A register reflects the field, mode and tenor of discourse; it is, as it were, a cross-section of all three of these types of variety. Thus in any given situation in which English is used, the user will adopt the register which he deems appropriate to that situation. He will often do this unconsciously: he will not stop to think, for example, whether it would be better to write a note to a casual acquaintance in the train than to speak to him. Choosing the register for a particular communication event is part of our competence as human beings, but it is also part of our native competence as speakers of the language that we can operate the chosen register in the right way. Throughout the course of a day you pick up and use a variety of registers: speaking at home over breakfast, going to work, addressing colleagues professionally, relaxing over coffee, writing business letters, and so on: each situation requires its own register. In the course of any period of everyday living you have to shift from one register to another, and this you do usually with very little thought. But shifting registers can sometimes be difficult. The person who 'talks like a book' may be someone who cannot easily adopt the appropriate register for the occasion and uses 'professional academic' language when he should be using 'informal conversational' language. Again, some people find themselves tongue-tied because they do not have (or *feel* that they do not have) control of the register required for a particular situation. Casual conversational language may be quite inappropriate, for example, for a serious professional discussion at a meeting or on radio.

In *The Five Clocks*, Martin Joos[98] characterizes this kind of language variety in accordance with a five-point scale. The *frozen* style is the formal, conventially correct English we use for severely objective transactional discourse; it is unlikely that frozen English would be used orally except when a text is being read aloud. The *formal* style is also correct in all respects, but it is less rigidly conventional, and it is often used, as for example in lectures, without being written-English-read-aloud. The *consultative* style is characteristically a spoken variety, used for professional (or otherwise non-casual) purposes. The *casual* style is used orally for ordinary everyday purposes between people who are behaving in a relaxed, casual manner. The *intimate* style is used among people who know one another well and who can be almost wholly indifferent about their choice of words, constructions and meanings. Each of these styles carries its own grammatical and lexical features.

In *English in Advertising*, Geoffrey Leech[99] employs a somewhat more refined set of categories. He sets out four 'polarities of style': *colloquial-formal, casual-ceremonial, personal-impersonal,* and *simple-complex*. For each of these dimensions of style he describes the circumstances which determine the choice of linguistic elements. The colloquial style is used for private purposes, and the formal style for public purposes. The most public of communication (for example, in official documents) is written without any regard to the person writing it or the person reading it as *individuals*: it is wholly objective, 'frozen'. There is, however, a 'public-colloquial' style which has been developed in more recent times to try to make formal communication more 'human': the English of 'high-quality' journalism and broadcasting exemplifies this style.

The *casual-ceremonial* dimension operates in private discourse, that is where the speaker or writer and the listener or reader are known to one another. The location you select for your language along the casual-ceremonial continuum will depend on your relationship with the person you are speaking to; in some languages you have to choose between familiar and impersonal pronouns, such as *tu* and *vous* in French and *du* and *Sie* in German; in English the choices are less direct but all the same there *are* choices to be made. One such choice has to do with the way in which you address a person: 'Yes, Mrs Brown' – 'Yes, Mary' – 'yes, honey' . . . . Another kind of choice is the amount of colloquial or slang words you use: 'Yes, Mrs Brown' – 'OK, Mary' – 'Yep, hon' . . . . But the choices involved are much more numerous and complex than these examples suggest: they include choice of grammar, choice of lexis, choice of meaning, choice of accent and many more.

The *personal-impersonal* dimension has to do with the amount of familiarity you wish to convey. One way of marking a very personal style is to use first and second person freely. In a wholly impersonal style, the first and second person pronouns will not appear at all. A slightly less impersonal effect is gained by the use of the 'editorial *we*': 'We may assume therefore' . . . . In a more personal style, the first person singular is used freely; another characteristic marker of 'personalness' is the use of the second person. (You will have noticed that I have tried to strike a personal tone in this book by using 'I' and 'you' quite often.) Another marker of the personal style is the use of a greater variety of sentence types than is found in impersonal styles: for example, to use more questions or exclamations will lend a more personal tone to the language.

The *simple-complex* dimension involves the amount of linguistic 'difficultness' involved in comprehending the message. Your choice of sentence grammar will be dictated to some extent, of course, by the subject matter and mode of discourse, but even within these circumstances you can locate your sentence construction along a continuum from simple to complex, as we have seen in Chapter 4 when discussing rhetoric. The contrast between simple and complex grammar available for the communication of the same message can be illustrated by examining the same news story in a 'popular' newspaper and in a 'quality' newspaper. This is not simply a question of the quantity of detail which is presented; it is a matter of deliberate and careful choice. One of the skills that must be learned by a journalist working on a tabloid paper is the construction of easy-to-read sentences. Another marker of the simple style as opposed to the complex style is the choice of vocabulary: the writer or speaker aiming at the simple style will avoid unusual words and will search for ways of conveying his message in familiar, widely know expressions. The more complex the style, the more demanding it will be on the reader's (or hearer's) ability to understand English, calling upon greater knowledge of English grammar, English lexis and English usage.

Correctness and Appropriateness

I have been at pains to describe the astonishing variety of dialects and diatypes which make up the linguistic phenomenon we call English. It should now be evident that the way we use English in any situation is determined by many interdependent influences. Different criteria must be employed to describe the English of any sample of the language. For each sample, the following questions must be asked:

Is it modern English or a temporal dialect?
Is it Standard English or non-Standard?
Which international variety of Standard English? or
Which dialect of non-Standard English?
What is the field of discourse?
What is the mode of discourse?
What is the tenor of discourse?
What is the style intended?

It is only after these questions have been answered that we can go on to discuss the *quality* or *effectiveness* of the language.

Chapter 4 discussed the grammatical and rhetorical features of *formal standard written English*. This is the kind of English that most people mean when they speak of 'good English'. The rules and conventions of English usage have preoccupied scholars for centuries. As we have seen, early scholars attempted to describe English in terms of Latin grammar, and produced 'rules' which, though suited to Latin, did not accurately correspond to the way English behaves. Similar efforts were made in the seventeenth century to produce rules for English usage, the way in which words are actually used in practice. Towards the end of the eighteenth century, however, the 'doctrine of usage' developed: the assertion that the most important criterion of language is what people actually do in 'good practice'. Although they often strayed away from the principles they professed, linguists such as Dr Johnson, Joseph Priestley and George Campbell established the view that 'general acceptation' (as Horace had put it long before) was 'the sole arbiter and norm of language'.[100]

Both before and since the doctrine of usage was promulgated, however, the didactic zeal of pundits has prevailed, especially in school course books. Many so-called rules have been pronounced, of the kind called 'ipsedixitisms': that is, rules that have no foundation except that some 'authority' has laid them down.[101] An *ipsedixitism* (the word is from Latin *ipse*, he himself, and *dixit*, he said) seems to survive by being taught in schools from one generation to another. One example, the *shall/will rule*, appears to have originated with John

Wallis, who wrote *Grammatica Linguae Anglicanae* in 1653. Although it has no basis in logic, and is not borne out by usage, the rule is still being taught. In a textbook still extant, for example, we are solemnly instructed thus:

Shall, Will – a. When simple future tense is intended, the following are the correct auxiliaries to use:

Singular	Plural
1st person, I shall.	We shall.
2nd person, Thou wilt (you will).	You will.
3rd person, He will.	They will.

b. When a promise, a threat or a command is intended, the following should be used:

Singular	Plural
1st person, I will.	We will.
2nd person, Thou shalt (you shall).	You shall.
3rd person, He shall.	They shall.[102]

Other ipsedixitisms were propounded by Robert Lowth in his *Short Introduction to English Grammar* in 1762. A famous example is his pronouncement that *than* is a conjunction, not a preposition, so that we should say 'He is fatter than I', not 'He is fatter than me'. Usage, in fact, belies this rule.

The reliance upon Latin grammar which the earlier pundits established is still influencing school textbook writers of the 'old school'. Because in Latin prepositions are preposed, John Dryden condemned the ending of a sentence with a preposition – an absurdity which, it is said, caused Winston Churchill to note in the margin 'This is the sort of English up with which I will not put'.[103] It is the Latin influence that makes some pundits deplore the use of *aggravate* to mean 'annoy', because the root *gravis* ought to make the word mean 'to make worse'. It is because of Latin, too, that some students are still being taught that English has a *gerund* (a noun formed from a verb ending in -*ing*) and that we must say 'excuse *my* asking' and 'He objected to *their* singing' and so on. We do not, of course, say these things in practice unless we have been conditioned to do so at school.

The truth is that in usage there is no single standard of acceptability. Every variety of English has its own peculiar conventions, options and standards. What may be adjudged 'wrong' in one generation may be widely accepted in another; what may be pronounced 'barbarous' or 'inelegant' by a self-styled authority may be universally used and tolerated in everyday practice; what may be urged as 'good English' in one part of the world may be calmly ignored in another.[104] Since each variety of English has its own structure, the effective use of English is a matter of making the grammatical and lexical choices which are appropriate to that variety. Just as we have to learn to shift into the appropriate register required for a particular situation, so we have to learn the rules and features of usage that best 'fit' the communication event we are operating within.

Some teachers confuse the notions of 'correctness' and 'appropriateness' because they are insufficiently aware of the variability of English. It is not a single, monolithic language; it changes as people's behaviour changes, because it *is* behaviour. Prescriptive rules as to what is proper in speech and writing are taught, out of ignorance, as if one set of rules can apply to any speech event or writing task. Old-fashioned course books are still prevalent in which pupils are drilled on 'do's' and 'don'ts' and expected to rationalize the cause of 'error' in terms of 'rules' which may be false or, at best, only partially applicable. Many usages are proscribed which are common in everyday speech and which may be actually required in certain varieties of English: forms such as 'It's me', 'Each of them have taken one', 'Who did you say you gave it to?' are universally used in colloquial styles of speech. The 'Correction of Errors' sections in these course books reveal their authors' misunderstanding of the nature of the English language. To require a student to 'correct' such sentences as *Excuse me being late, I rose late so I had to hurry, The man only died yesterday* is to show ignorance as to the difference between the uses of English in different situations.[105] Sentences like those are colloquial; they would hardly ever occur in the kind of prose in which the 'rules' they are thought to disobey are relevant. They are all 'correct' in appropriate contexts. They might be translated into different registers, but they need not be 'corrected' for the contexts in which they are appropriate.

This state of confusion has resulted from the establishment of Standard English as the preferred dialect of English throughout the world: this has become the language of educated, cultivated native speakers. To say that *I seen him* is incorrect is equivalent to saying that the form does not occur in SE, which prefers *I saw him*. To say that *It's me* is incorrect, on the other hand, is equivalent to saying that speakers of SE would never use that form – and that is not so. *It's me* is a standard form in SE, but it would not be appropriate in *formal written SE*. To condemn 'the nob's pronoun' as used in *Between you and I* or *It's from Jim and I* is foolish when popular usage seems likely to make it acceptable in colloquial registers, but it is still to be avoided in formal registers.

The search for objectivity in modern linguistics has led some writers to assert that it is improper to apply prescriptions of any kind to the use of English. Robert A. Hall, Jr.'s book, *Leave Your Language Alone*,[106] is a good example of this extreme attitude. Some of Hall's assertions, which he calls 'basic principles', have become familiar in educational discussion:

> There is no such thing as good and bad (or correct and incorrect, grammatical and ungrammatical, right and wrong) in language. All languages and dialects are of equal merit, each in its own way.
> 'Correct' can only mean 'socially acceptable' and apart from this has no meaning as applied to language.

As it reads, the proposition that 'there is no such thing as correct and incorrect, grammatical and ungrammatical etc.' is manifestly nonsense: no linguist would deny that *The kicks balls boys the* is ungrammatical and therefore incorrect. What Hall really means, of course, is that the linguist is not concerned with how people ought to speak but is interested in all language uses, whether socially acceptable or not; and that *within its own rules* any dialect of English is just as rule-governed as any other.

Nevertheless, to say that there is no ineluctable measure of correctness in English is not to say that there is never a right–wrong opposition. Of course there are many contexts in which one form is wrong and another correct. In the technical sense, grammaticality affords yes/no judgements which native speakers could not question. The rules of English rhetoric are, in the main, fairly well established and described. In questions of usage we must have recourse to the evidence of the majority to show what is generally deemed to be 'acceptable', but at any given time there is usually a consensus among the educated users of English. But what is 'right' in any situation is what is most *appropriate*. The language that best fits the needs of the speaker or writer, that best meets the requirements of the situation, the subject at hand, the listener or reader, is the 'right' language. The most useful basis for judgements of the quality or effectiveness of English is its suitability for the task it is called upon to perform.

Standards: What is Good English?[107]

Complaints that students lack the 'basic skills' of English are not new: every official report since 1900 in both Britain and America seems to have reiterated expressions of dissatisfaction with the standards of literacy being achieved. Every decade of the present century has seen the launching of some project designed to improve people's ability to use English. Recent years have witnessed even more strenuous complaints and strongly expressed criticisms of the effectiveness of English teaching. Every report or critical speech, however, also bears witness to the ignorance of many people about language and language learning. Complaints about 'standards' are irritating and disconcerting to those of us whose professional lives are devoted to the improvement of English teaching. We are inclined to point out that people tend to misunderstand the nature of linguistic competence, and that it all depends on what you mean by 'basic skills', 'standards' and so on. Accusations call forth counter-accusations: the laity fail to provide teachers with the resources they need to teach English properly; teachers are fighting a losing battle against the indifference of parents and the time-consuming ravages of television, and so on.

Employers, examiners, and teachers of other subjects have every right to ask whether English teaching is as effective as it might be, and whether the standards of proficiency being attained are sufficient for the requirements of a modern industrial society. Many teachers of English are themselves uncertain about what they should do to improve matters. To make matters worse, teachers of English are not unanimous about what their subject should set out to do. One school of thought perceives English, as a subject, as one of the Humanities, an enculturating discipline whose main objectives are to develop social and 'life' competencies through language activities such as reading and discussion and self-expression in speech and writing. Another school of thought would argue that all schooling has these objectives, but English teaching uniquely deals with language and the uses of language. These positions are not in direct opposition, but almost every teacher exhibits a bias toward either pole in the content and style of his teaching.

One difficulty which bedevils the teaching of English is that teachers have no recognized methods of assessing the quality of a pupil's language or of estimating the general standards of proficiency from one age group to the next. For their own pupils' progress, the subjective judgement of an efficient teacher may be good enough in the elementary stages of schooling. Provided they are knowledgeable and well trained, teachers can apply a personal inventory of criteria to estimate how an individual is performing as against others in the group and in accordance with his own potential; by this means, from seeing him in action day by day, the teacher can decide what, and in what ways, each child needs to learn. Apart from reading tests, however, there is no means of comparing one generation's linguistic proficiency with that of any other. At the secondary stage, the teacher has even less to work with. Seeing the pupil infrequently, they cannot, like their colleague at the primary stages, rely on careful, prolonged observation. They must fall back on tests devised and administered in artificial conditions.

Even tests are unsatisfactory for most purposes. Despite some important research, we have no feasible way of measuring competence in talk or listening.[108] There has been an enormous quantity of research into the measurement of reading attainment, but no incontrovertible measurements have been established to show how one pupil, or group, or age cohort compares with another. Even the efficacy of reading tests is highly controverted. No widely accepted means of assessing competence in writing has ever been found; and the notion of 'competence' has never been defined to the satisfaction of many educators. In respect of the kind of skill measuring which would genuinely aid the teacher in his classroom, diagnostic assessment, research is still in its infancy.

If objective or scientific measurements of attainment in the English skills are unsatisfactory, how much credence can be given to the subjective opinions of employers, journalists, writers of letters to the press? The researcher at least has some objective notion of what he is trying to measure. What he measures may not be widely acceptable as true indicators of language competence. We may argue that his definition of reading or writing is narrow and even in varying degree irrelevant. But the layman's ideas of standards are so confused that it is difficult even to begin improving his understanding without a lengthy consideration of the nature of language in education. The subject of 'good English' has been obscured for generations by false beliefs, unfounded assertions and mistaken assumptions. Much blame for this can be attached to teachers themselves, especially those who produce and use the textbooks that perpetuate the myths of 'basic skills', 'correctness', and so on.

As we have seen, the notion of 'correctness' has it that English is monolithic, having a central 'good' form and various 'bad' forms accreting to which are innumerable 'errors' which have to be 'corrected'. This conception of a supreme, standard form of 'good English' seems to embrace every level of language. At the phonological level, 'good' means RP, or the sound-system of the educated upper-class Bostonian, or the 'cultivated Australian' accent. At the level of grammar and usage, 'good' means the sentence syntax and vocabulary of formal written SE. At the level of lexis, 'good' means the diction of formal SE, and the absence of colloquialisms, slang and other 'improprieties'. At the level of style, 'good' can only mean 'what *I* like', but it often means the style of some respected 'classic' writers like Addison or Emerson. As we have seen, too, correctness is believed to be achievable by adherence to a known set of rules, which are embedded in textbooks and in the work of certain respected pundits such as Fowler's *Modern English Usage* and Sir Ernest Gower's *Plain Words*.[109]

It is not generally realized that errors in grammar are not, in fact, the principal faults of poor writing in English. Of course the inadequately taught writer will commit errors in sentence construction. Most of us make errors of a similar kind in our casual speech – for example, losing track of the subject in a long sentence, or selecting the wrong number for a verb, or getting a participial phrase related illogically. In talk we generally ignore these errors in our own speech and in that of others; but almost every native speaker of English can make well-formed utterances by the age of ten. What characterizes poor English composition is not bad grammar but poor eloquence and inadequate mastery of the tricks of rhetoric.

The doctrine of multiple standards recognizes that there is no single form of English suitable for all occasions and all situations. The efficient teacher will nowadays emphasize the role of appropriatenesss: the best English for a particular job is the English that most successfully fits the situation and performs the intended function. Thus the teacher must aim at giving the pupil linguistic versatility – the capability of writing and speaking in different ways to suit different purposes. The ancient art of rhetoric should still be the preoccupation of the teacher of advanced English. It is unfortunate that so many teachers know so little of rhetoric and are themselves so weak as practitioners of the art.

To asseverate that traditional notions of correctness are naive is not to say that there are no standards of good English. It is important that pupils should become proficient in the use of the varieties of English required for life and work in the modern world. Different skills are needed for various Englishes: for formal intellectual discourse, for consultative exchange, for job reports, business letters and a thousand other situations. There is a fairly narrow range of styles which are important in professional and social life, and no responsible teacher will consciously neglect the teaching of these skills. Underlying all these different Englishes and styles, too, there is a core of rulebound linguistic habits which can properly be called general competence.

The *basic* skills of good English, however, are not the surface, clerical skills that easily catch the eye – handwriting, spelling, punctuation, accuracy in sentence grammar. These are only the outer garments of competence. What makes communication effective is, firstly, its content, the information or ideas or feelings it conveys. Whatever the true relationship between thought and language, one will pay more attention to the meaning of an utterance than its form. Secondly, effective communication requires a skilful choice of language, in the form of lexis and grammar, so selected that the meaning is transmitted in the way intended. To be effective, some writing or speech should be transparent, wholly unobtrusive; but other examples might require that the language be clamantly evident to the senses of the receiver.

Much poor English can be attributed to sheer poverty of vocabulary. We all have to acquire a wordhoard which includes the vocabularies we need for the tasks we use English to accomplish: our effectiveness as communicators depends on the vocabularies we command. The efficient teacher will try hard to help the pupils in the long, slow process of acquiring vocabulary. This is achieved by being *involved* with words, by using them and experiencing their message in situations where their power can be genuinely felt.

Another basic requirement for good English is 'sentence sense': the ability to construct a sentence that efficiently carries the intended message. This ability cannot come from routine drilling. It is a long process of learning that leads to it, a process of becoming intuitively sensitive and skilled with words and patterns. 'Mastery' comes of continuous experience. But 'mastery' is a relative term: there can be no standard of perfection, no stage at which there is no more to learn.

There is, finally, a truth about good English that must be appreciated by all who learn and teach the language. This is that English is a huge and complex phenomenon and difficult to learn. Although English is a relatively easy language for a foreigner to learn adequately for common purposes, English as a means of communication is a difficult accomplishment. People testify to this by their continuing interest in cheap and easy ways to develop their English. But there are no cheap and easy ways. It requires a massive investment of time and energy to acquire even a modest degree of mastery in English: time spent talking, reading, writing, studying – hour upon hour, year after year. Above all, perhaps, it requires the motivation to make that investment: the impulse towards using the language that comes of enjoying it and what it can do. You learn English by using it.

Conclusion

You learn English by using it. This is the message of my book. Using language by reading, writing, listening, talking, is the best and only

way to acquire the skills of communication. I hope my book has
helped you toward a better understanding of this simple, but yet
radically important, truth.

Notes and References

1 The Nature of Language

1. This famous example was first used by John Crowe Ransom in *The World's Body*, New York, 1938.
2. By M. A. K. Halliday, in Angus McIntosh and M. A. K. Halliday, *Patterns of Language*, Longman, 1966, p. 3.
3. Otto Jespersen, *Language: Its Nature, Development & Origin*, Allen & Unwin, 1922.
4. Grammatically, verbals like *drawing, entering* and so on could be substituted for *in*, but this would change the logic of the sentence in a way that the substitution of a preposition would not. The set of words of which *drawing, entering* and so on are members is an open one: that is, you could keep on inventing verbals that fit the slot.
5. In this section I draw freely from the following sources:
   'Semantics', by Manfred Bierwisch, in John Lyons (ed.), *New Horizons in Linguistics*, Penguin Books, 1970
   Geoffrey Leech, *Semantics*, Penguin Books, 1976
   'Semantics and Language Teaching', by Paul Van Buren, in J. P. B. Allen and S. Pit Corder (eds.) *Papers in Applied Linguistics*, OUP, 1976.
   However, these authors provide a scholarly introduction to the subject while I merely give a brief indication of what the subject deals with. Readers interested in studying semantics seriously are recommended to begin with John Lyons, *Structural Semantics*, Blackwell, 1963, and Geoffrey Leech, *Towards a Semantic Description of English*, Longman, 1969.
6. J. R. Firth, *The Tongues of Men*, OUP, 1964.

2 The Development of Communicative Competence

7. For an excellent critical account of this learning theory as it applies to language see Ruth Clark's chapter in J. P. B. Allen and S. Pit Corder (eds.), *Papers in Applied Linguistics*, OUP, 1975.
8. Chomsky's review of Skinner's *Verbal Behavior* (Appleton-Century-Crofts, 1957) was published in *Language*, 35, pp. 26–58, 1959, and in J. A. Fodor and J. J. Katz (eds.), *The Structure of Language*, Prentice Hall, 1964.
9. For a more detailed account of this theory, see my essay 'Language and

Education', in M. Marland, *Language Across the Curriculum*, Heinemann, 1977.

10. Chomsky's grammatical theories were presented in his *Syntactic Structures*, Mouton, 1957, and *Aspects of the Theory of Syntax*, MIT Press, 1965. For a simpler exposition of TG Grammar, see H. A. Gleason, Jr. *Linguistics and English Grammar*, Holt, Rinehart and Winston, 1965.

11. For an excellent account of early language learning, see Jean Aitchison, *The Articulate Mammal*, Hutchinson, 1978. A brief and lucid account is given in E. C. Stork and J. D. A. Widdowson, *Learning About Linguistics*, Hutchinson, 1974.

12. For recent theoretical discussions of this subject see J. S. Bruner and K. J. Connolly, *The Development of Competence in Early Childhood*, Academic Press, 1976; J. P. B. Allen and S. Pit Corder (eds.), op cit.; A. Davies (ed.), *Language and Learning in Early Childhood*, Heinemann, 1977.

13. These case histories are described in R. Brown, *Words and Things*, Free Press, 1958; *Language*, 50, 1974; and Jean Aitchison, op. cit.

14. See my essay, 'Language and Education', in M. Marland, op. cit.; also P. Trudgill, *Sociolinguistics*, Penguin, 1975.

15. J. S. Bruner, *The Relevance of Education*, Allen and Unwin, 1971, p. 141.

16. More detailed accounts of Piaget's theories can be found in: D. G. Boyle, *Language and Thinking in Human Development*, Hutchinson, 1971; J. P. B. Allen and S. Pit Corder (eds.), op. cit.; Mary Ann Pulaski, *Understanding Piaget*, Harper & Row, 1971; B. Inhelder and H. H. Chipman (eds.), *Piaget and his School*, Springer-Verlag, 1976; also various articles in the journals *Child Development* and *The New Era*; Julia Solomon, *Learning to Think*, Kindergarten Association of Western Australia, 1973, offers an account from the viewpoint of nursery education; and Margaret Donaldson, *Children's Minds*, Fontana, 1978, gives a lucid critical analysis by an authority on child development.

17. L. S. Vygotsky, *Thought and Language*, MIT Press, 1962.

18. J. S. Bruner, *Toward a Theory of Instruction*, Harvard University Press, 1966.

19. J. S. Bruner, 'Language as an Instrument of Thought', in A. Davies (ed.), *Problems of Language and Learning*, Heinemann, 1975.

20. Ruth Weir, *Language in the Crib*, Mouton, 1962.

21. See D. McNeill, 'Developmental Psycholinguistics' in F. Smith and G. A. Miller (eds.), *The Genesis of Language*, MIT Press, 1966; and D. McNeill, *The Acquisition of Language*, Harper & Row, 1970.

22. J. Dore, cited in Malcolm Coulthard, *An Introduction to Discourse Analysis*, Longman, 1977.

23. See my essay, 'Language and Education' in M. Marland, op. cit., p. 51.

24. Joan Tough, *The Development of Meaning*, Allen & Unwin, 1977.

3 The Development of Language Skills

25. For some of my material on discourse I have drawn upon M. Coulthard, *An Introduction to Discourse Analysis*, Longman, 1977.

26. For what follows I have drawn, among other sources, upon D. B. Fry, 'Speech Reception and Perception', and P. N. Johnson-Laird, 'The Reception and Memory of Sentences', both in J. Lyons (ed.), *New Horizons in Linguistics*, Penguin, 1970.

27. This example is cited by D. B. Fry from C. E. Shannon, 'Prediction and Entropy of Printed English', *Bell System Technical Journal*, 1950. Information theory has contributed valuably to our understanding of communicative processes, both of speech and reading.

28. An excellent source of games and activities is *Language Development and the Disadvantaged Child,* published for the Schools Council by Holmes McDougall, 1978. Since all children are 'disadvantaged' in respect of oral training, this book can be recommended to all teachers of young pupils.

29. Much attention has been paid recently to the production of classroom materials designed to further pupils' knowledge of how language works. The Schools Council's Programme in Linguistics and English Teaching (started in 1964 under the aegis of the Nuffield Foundation, the Department of Education and Science and the Scottish Education Programme) has produced some excellent guidance for teachers. *Language in Use* by Peter Doughty, John Pearce and Geoffrey Thornton (Arnold, 1971) provides teachers with a large number of teaching strategies and ideas. *Language and Communication,* by Ian Forsyth and Kathleen Wood (Longman, 1977) is an English language course for younger secondary pupils. Open University courses and publications offer excellent guidance.

30. B. B. Hudgins, *The Instructional Process*, Rand McNally, 1971.

31. See, for example, D. Barnes, *Language, the Learner and the School,* Penguin, 1971; also M. Marland (ed.), *Language Across the Curriculum,* Heinemann, 1977; and *A Language for Life,* (the Bullock Report), HMSO, 1975.

32. Edward Sapir (1884–1939) was a leading American scholar who valuably influenced the growth of linguistics with such books as *Language* (Harcourt Bruce and World, 1921).

33. In this section, I draw heavily from a paper I wrote for the United Kingdom Reading Association 'Developing Reading Efficiencies', in M. Clark, and A. Milne (eds.), *Reading and Related Skills*, Ward Lock, 1973. Other sources are Frank Smith's brilliant, if idiosyncratic, study, *Understanding Reading,* Holt, Rinehart & Winston, 1971; and H. Levin and Joanna P. Williams (eds.), *Basic Studies on Reading*, Basic Books Inc., 1970.

34. This model is described by Kenneth Goodman, a pioneer of the psycholinguistic explanation of reading. (K. S. Goodman, 'Reading: a Psycholinguistic Guessing Game', in *Journal of the Reading Specialist, 6,* USA, May 1968.)

35. A. K. Pugh, *Silent Reading*, Heinemann, 1978.

36. U. Neisser, *Cognitive Psychology*, Appleton-Century-Crofts, 1967.

37. J. Hochberg, *Basic Studies on Reading*, Basic Books Inc., 1970.

38. Paul A. Kolers, op. cit.

39. For an interesting study of this activity see Kenyon Calthrop, *Reading Together*, Heinemann, 1971.

40. See the work of Ruth Strickland, *The Language of Elementary School Children*, University of Indiana, 1962; Walter Loban, *The Language of Elementary School Children*, NCTE, Champaign, Illinois, 1963, and *Problems in Oral English*, NCTE, Champaign, Illinois, 1966; Kellog Hunt, *Grammatical Structures at Three Grade Levels,* NCTE, Champaign, Illinois, 1963; R. Braddock, R. Lloyd Jones and L. Schoer, *Research in Written Composition,* NCTE, Champaign, Illinois, 1963; J. Britton *et al.*, *The Development of Writing Abilities (11–18)*, Macmillan, 1975; N. Martin, P. D'Arcy, B. Newton and R. Parker, *Writing and Learning Across the Curriculum 11–16*, Ward Lock Educational, 1976; *Writing Across the Curriculum Project*, Ward Lock Educational, 1976; C. Burgess *et al.*, *Understanding Children Writing*, Penguin, 1973.

41. See, for example, an essay by the anthropologist Edmund Leach, *Literacy*, issued by The Nevis Institute, Edinburgh, 1977.

42. See M. A. K. Halliday, A. McIntosh, and P. Strevens, *The Linguistic Sciences and Language Teaching*, Longman, 1964.

43. This example is from H. A. Gleason, Jr., *Linguistics and English Grammar*, Holt, Rinehart and Winston, 1965.

44. *Breakthrough to Literacy*, developed by D. Mackay, Brian Thompson and Pamela Schaub for the Schools Council Programme in Linguistics and English Teaching, an initial reading and writing series published by Longman.

45. James Britton, 'Teaching Writing', in A. Davies (ed.), *Problems of Language and Learning*, Heinemann, 1975.

46. This distinction was first suggested by D. W. Harding in 'The role of the onlooker', *Scrutiny*, VI (3), 1937.

47. This and some other observations in these paragraphs are from James Britton's Essay 'Teaching Writing', in A. Davies (ed.), *Problems of Language and Learning*, Heinemann, 1975. In the same volume I contribute a discussion of Britton's scheme in which I pose some questions as to its relevance to the *process* of writing.

48. For further descriptions of these categories, see J. Britton *et al.*, *The Development of Writing Abilities 11–18*, Macmillan, 1975, and Nancy Martin in M. Marland (ed.) *Language Across the Curriculum*, Heinemann, 1977.

49. This brilliant application was first proposed by Robert Zoellner, Colorado State University, in *College English*, NCTE, Champaign, Illinois, January, 1969.

50. These and many other notes in this section are drawn from the work of Richard L. Venezky, particularly *The Structure of English Orthography*, Mouton, 1970 and 'Regularity in Reading and Spelling' in *Basic Studies on Reading*, Basic Books Inc., 1970. But Venezky is not responsible for my general observations and deductions about the pedagogy of spelling. I have also consulted D. G. Scragg, *A History of English Spelling*, Manchester University Press, 1975.

51. This poem, apparently by someone with the initials TSW, was published as part of a letter from a J. Bland in the *Sunday Times*, 3 January, 1965.

52. R. L. Venezky, *The Structure of English Orthography*, Mouton, 1970.

53. R. L. Venezky, op. cit., p. 30.

54. In *Pygmalion* ('Note for Technicians'), Penguin, 1941.

55. R. L. Venezky, op. cit., p. 32.

56. Felicia Lamport, 'Dictionaries: Our Language Right or Wrong', in *Words, Words and Words about Dictionaries,* Jack C. Gray (ed.), Chandler Publishing, San Francisco, 1963.

4 Grammar, Rhetoric and Diction

57. C. C. Fries, *The Structure of English*, Harcourt Brace, 1952; H. Whitehall, *Structural Essentials of English*, Longman, 1958; P. Roberts, *Patterns of English* and *English Sentences*, Harcourt Brace, 1956 and 1962; R. Quirk, *The Use of English*, Longman, 1962; B. Strang, *Modern English Structure*, Edward Arnold, 1962; W. H. Mittins, *A Grammar of Modern English*, Methuen, 1962. For accounts of the development of school grammars see H. A. Gleason, Jr., *Linguistics and English Grammar*, Holt, Rinehart and Winston, 1965, and W. B. Currie, *New Directions in Teaching English Language*, Longman, 1973. My own essay, 'Language and Education', in M. Marland (ed.) *Language Across the Curriculum*, Heinemann, 1977, contains some relevant discussion.

58. See, for example, various publications issued since 1928 by the National Council of Teachers of English, Champaign, Illinois.

59. See, for example, the bulletins of the Central Committee on English, particularly *The Teaching of English Language*, HMSO, 1972, and various issues of *Teaching English*, the journal published by the Centre for Information on Teaching English, Edinburgh.

60. Although the grammar offered here is a presentation of my own, I have drawn freely from the following: H. A. Gleason, Jr., *Linguistics and English Grammar*, Holt, Rinehart and Winston, 1965; Marshall L. Brown, Elmer G. White and Edward B. Jenkinson, *Two Approaches to Teaching Syntax*, Indiana University Press, 1967; Owen Thomas, *Transformational Grammar and the Teaching of English*, Holt, Rinehart and Winston, 1965; and my own essay, 'Language and Education' in M. Marland (ed.) *Language Across the Curriculum*, Heinemann, 1977.

61. By G. Campbell, in *The Philosophy of Rhetoric*, 1776. This quotation is from W. B. Currie, *New Directions in Teaching English Language,* Longman, 1973, from which I have drawn some of the material for this section. In this section I have also made use of the *Harbrace College Handbook,* Harcourt Brace, 1956, which still contains much excellent guidance on composition. Another useful book for this purpose is Robert Graves and Alan Hodge *The Reader Over Your Shoulder*, Cape, 1943: though dated, it is entertaining and authoritative.

62. This is quoted from a column in *The New Statesman* called 'This English' which was devoted to printing examples of bad English sent in by readers.

63. This is from Robert Graves and Alan Hodge, op. cit., pp. 149–50.

64. The first quotation is from Barrett Wendell *English Composition*, first published in 1890, and the second from Francis Christensen, 'A Generative Rhetoric of the Paragraph' in *College Composition and Communication*, NCTE, Champaign, Illinois, October 1965. Both cited in Paul C. Rodgers, Jr., 'A Discourse-Centered Rhetoric of the Paragraph' in *College Composition and Communication,* February 1966.

65. Paul C. Rodgers, Jr., op. cit., p. 6.

66. Introduction to *Webster's Collegiate Thesaurus*, G. and C. Merriam Company, Springfield Mass., 1976.

67. In 'Politics and the English Language', *Collected Essays*, Mercury, 1961.

68. G. N. Leech, *A Linguistic Guide to English Poetry*, Longman, 1969.

69. From *Sullivan at Bay* (Dent), quoted in Guy Pocock and M. M. Bozman (ed.), *Modern Humour*, Dent, 1940.

5. The Englishes of the World.

70. The best short account of dialects available is in Michael Gregory and Susanne Carroll, *Language and Situation*, Routledge and Kegan Paul, 1978. Other useful sources of information are: Richard W. Bailey and Jay L. Robinson, *Varieties of Present-day English*, Macmillan, 1973; J. B. Pride and Janet Holmes (eds.), *Sociolinguistics*, Penguin, 1974; Peter Trudgill, *Sociolinguistics*, Penguin, 1975.

71. For a concise history of the rise of Standard English, see Albert C. Baugh and Thomas Cable, *A History of the English Language*, Routledge and Kegan Paul, 1978, pp. 191–6.

72. See Raven McDavid, Jr., in *American Social Dialects,* NCTE, Champaign, Illinois, 1965, and in 'Go Slow in Ethnic Attributions: Geographic Mobility and Dialect Prejudices' in Richard W. Bailey and Jay L. Robinson (eds.), *Varieties of Present-Day English*, Macmillan, 1973.

73. N. Mitford (ed.), *Noblesse Oblige*, Hamish Hamilton, 1956. Ross's contribution, 'U and Non-U: an Essay in Sociological Linguistics', reiterated findings in his earlier essay 'Linguistic Class Indicators in Present-Day English', in *Neuphilologische Mitteilungen,* Helsinki, 1954.

74. William Labov, *The Social Stratification of English in New York City*, Center for Applied Linguistics, Washington DC, 1966; *The Logic of Non-Standard English*, Georgetown University Press, 1970; *Language in the Inner City*, Conduct and Communications No. 3, Philadelphia, 1972; *Sociolinguistic Patterns*, University of Pennsylvania Press, 1972. See also R. K. S. Macaulay, *Language, Social Class and Education,* Edinburgh University Press, 1977; Peter Trudgill, *The Social Differentiation of English in Norwich*, Cambridge University Press, 1974.

75. See, for example, Muriel Crosby's essay in *Reading and the Language Arts*, University of Chicago Press, 1963, where she refers to such experiments held in Wilmington, Delaware, USA.

76. For a demonstration of the grammaticality of the double negative in Black American English, see Jay L. Robinson, 'The Wall of Babel', in R. W. Bailey and J. L. Robinson (eds.), *Varieties of Present-Day English*, Macmillan, 1973.

77. P. Trudgill, *Sociolinguistics*, Penguin, 1975, p. 40 ff.

78. Angus McIntosh, *Introduction to a Survey of Scottish Dialects*, Nelson, 1961.

79. See Albert C. Baugh and Thomas Cable, op. cit.

80. An excellent little book by Peter Strevens, *British and American English*, Cassell, 1978, provides brief accounts of most of the topics dealt with in this section. See also A. C. Baugh, and Thomas Cable, op. cit., p. 351 ff.

81. These examples are drawn from Peter Strevens, op. cit. p. 50. Strevens, however, does not show any distinction between SEE and SSE.

82. In *The Listener*, 14 December, 1978.

83. *Mountain English*, Tarmac Audio Visual Co., North Carolina, undated.

84. See Walter A. Wolfram, William Labov, Raven I. McDavid, Jr. and Roger W. Shuy in R. W. Bailey and J. L. Robinson (eds.), *Varieties of Present-Day English*, Macmillan, 1973.

85. A. G. Mitchell, 'The Australian Accent'; J. S. Gunn, 'Twentieth Century Australian Idiom'; G. K. W. Johnston, 'The Language of Australian Literature'; all these are in W. S. Ramson (ed.), *English Transported*, Australian National University Press, 1970.

86. A. Delbridge, 'The Recent Study of Spoken Australian English', in W. S. Ramson, op. cit.

87. J. A. W. Bennett, 'English as it is Spoken in New Zealand', in W. S. Ramson, op. cit., p. 70 ff; see also G. W. Turner, 'New Zealand and English Today', in the same volume.

88. See Kenneth Ramchand, 'The Language of the Master?' in R. W. Bailey and Jay L. Robinson, op. cit., p. 115 ff.

89. F. G. Cassidy, 'Jamaica Talk', quoted in R. W. Bailey and Jay L. Robinson, op. cit., p. 129 ff.

90. See D. Hopwood, *South African English Pronunciation*, Cape Town, 1928; L. W. Lanham, *The Pronunciation of South African English*, Cape Town, 1967, cited in Albert C. Baugh and Thomas Cable, op. cit.

91. L. W. Lanham, 'Teaching English to Africans: a Crisis in Education', in *Optima*, Johannesburg, December 1965.

6. The Uses of English

92. For this section I have drawn upon Michael Gregory and Susanne Carroll's excellent little book, *Language and Situation*, Routledge and Kegan Paul, 1978.

93. This term was first proposed by the anthropologist Malinowski in C. K. Ogden and I. A. Richards (eds.), *The Meaning of Meaning*, Routledge, 1946.

94. S. I. Hayakawa, *Language in Thought and Action*, Harcourt Brace, 1949.

95. John Betjeman, 'The Executive', John Murray, 1974.

96. From *The Guardian*, 26 July 1978.

97. See Geoffrey N. Leech, *English in Advertising,* Longman, 1966.

98. Martin Joos, *The Five Clocks,* Indiana University Press, 1962.

99. Geoffrey N. Leech, op. cit.

100. See Albert C. Baugh and Thomas Cable, *A History of the English Language,* Routledge and Kegan Paul, 1978.

101. See W. H. Mittins, 'What is correctness?' in A. Wilkinson (ed.) *The State of Language,* University of Birmingham, 1969.

102. J. Barclay and D. H. Knox, *Approach to Standard English,* Gibson, 1958.

103. E. Gowers, *The Complete Plain Words,* HMSO, 1954.

104. See my essay, 'Language and Education', in M. Marland (ed.) *Language Across the Curriculum,* Heinemann, 1977.

105. A. M. Philp, *Attitudes to Correctness in English,* Longman, 1968.

106. Revised as *Linguistics and Your Language,* Doubleday, 1960.

107. In this section I have drawn from my article 'Good English: Some Simple Truths', in *The Times Educational Supplement,* 21 September 1973.

108. See *A Language for Life* (the Bullock Report), HMSO, 1975.

109. H. W. Fowler, *Modern English Usage,* was first published by the OUP in 1926 and has appeared in many subsequent editions. Gowers' books, *Plain Words* and *The A.B.C. of Plain Words* etc. were published by HMSO in the 1940s and 1950s.

Select Bibliography for Further Study

(These lists are set out under the Chapter headings of the book. Some books appear more than once because they offer different topics.)

1. The Nature of Language

General

1. Allen, J. P. B. and Pit Corder, S. (eds.) *Papers in Applied Linguistics,* OUP, 1975. Excellent introductory studies for teachers.
2. Black, Max, *The Labyrinth of Language,* Pall Mall Press, London, 1968. An excellent account of the nature of language written for the non-specialist, with chapters on 'Thoughts and Language' and 'The Meaning of Meaning'.
3. Crystal, David, *Linguistics*, Penguin, 1977. First published 1971. An authoritative academic exposition. Requires serious effort of study.
4. Firth, J. R., *The Tongues of Men and Speech,* OUP, 1964. Early essays by the father of British linguistics. Worth reading if you are already familiar with the subject.
5. Girdansky, Michael, *The Adventure of Language*, Allen and Unwin, London, 1963; Prentice-Hall, USA, 1963. A brilliant popular account of the nature and development of language.
6. Hall, Robert A., Jr., *Linguistics and Your Language*, Anchor Books, Doubleday, New York, 1960. First published in 1950 as *Leave Your Language Alone*. A provocative introduction to the 'new ideas'. Now partly out-dated. Still worth reading.
7. Halliday, M. A. K., McIntosh, Angus and Strevens, Peter, *The Linguistic Sciences and Language Teaching*, Longman, 1964. An important introduction for teachers of English to native speakers or foreigners.
8. Laird, Charlton, *Thinking About Language*, Holt, Rinehart, and Winston, New York, 1961. A brief but lucid essay on modern views of language, including words, grammar, usage.
9. McIntosh, Angus and Halliday, M. A. K., *Patterns of Language*, Longman, 1966. Informative and interesting essays for the specializing student.
10. Potter, Simeon, *Modern Linguistics*, Deutsch, 1957. Somewhat out-of-date but still a useful account of phonology and vocabulary.

11. Quirk, Randolph, *The Use of English*, Longman, 1962. Excellent simple introduction to linguistic concepts relevant to teaching.
12. Quirk, Randolph. *The Study of the Mother Tongue*, H. K. Lewis, 1961. Worthwhile reading – Professor Quirk's inaugural lecture.
13. Robins, R. H., *General Linguistics*, Longman, 1964. Thorough and comprehensive academic study of linguistic science.
14. Stork, E. C. and Widdowson, J. D. A., *Learning About Linguistics*, Hutchinson, 1974. A good introductory workbook for the serious student.
15. Strevens, P. D., *The Study of the Present-Day English Language*, Leeds University Press, 1963. Professor Strevens' inaugural lecture, worth reading as an introduction to the study of contemporary English.

Specialist

16. Leech, Geoffrey, *Semantics*, Penguin, 1974. A first-rate introduction to a difficult subject.
17. Lyons, John, (ed.) *New Horizons in Linguistics*, Penguin, 1970. An important collection of technical studies.
18. Lyons, John, *Chomsky*, Fontana, 1970. Lucid introduction to Chomsky's work as linguist and philosopher.
19. Pride, J. B., and Holmes, Janet, (eds.), *Sociolinguistics*, Penguin, 1974. Readings on linguistic change, varieties, etc. Requires technical knowledge.
20. *Programme in Linguistics and English Teaching*: Lushington, Stephen (ed.), *Introductory Reading Lists*, Longman, 1968. Useful bibliography, though dated. Davies, Eirian, *Aspects of General Linguistics*, Excellent but highly technical introductory sketch.
21. Strang, Barbara M. H., *Modern English Structure*, Edward Arnold, 1962. A comprehensive account of English phonology and grammar.
22. Trudgill, Peter, *Sociolinguistics*, Penguin, 1974. An excellent introduction.
23. *Word* (Journal of the Linguistic Circle of New York), Vol. 17, No. 3, December 1961. Contains M. A. K. Halliday's important 'Categories of the Theory of Grammar'.

Historical

24. Baugh, Albert C. and Cable, Thomas. *A History of the English Language*, Routledge and Kegan Paul, 1978. This is the third edition, the first being by Baugh in 1935. A classic.
25. Jespersen, Otto, *Language: Its Nature, Development and Origin*, Allen and Unwin, 1922. Still worth reading despite being dated.
26. Palmer, L. R., *An Introduction to Modern Linguistics*, Macmillan, 1936. Useful for historical sections.

2. The Development of Communicative Competence

The Theory of Language Acquisition.

General

1. Boyle, D. G., *Language and Thinking in Human Development*, Hutchinson, 1971. An excellent simplified introduction.
2. De Cecco, John P., *The Psychology of Language, Thought and Instruction*, Holt, Rinehart and Winston, 1969. Readings from Vygotsky, Whorf, Sapir, Skinner, Chomsky, Piaget and others.

Specialist

3. Chomsky, Noam, *Review of Skinner's Verbal Behaviour, Language*, 35, 1959; and in Foder, J. A., and Katz, J. J., (eds.), *The Structure of Language*, Prentice Hall, 1964.
4. Chomsky, Noam, *Language and Mind*, Harcourt Brace, 1972. Difficult but worthwhile.
5. Moore, T. E., (ed.), *Cognitive Development and the Acquisition of Language*, Academic Press, New York, 1973. Important collection of studies.
6. Oldfield, R. C., and Marshall, J. C. (eds.), *Language*, Penguin, 1968. Useful theoretical readings.
7. Skinner, B. F., *Verbal Behavior*, Appleton-Century-Crofts, 1957. Closely argued, highly technical, but illuminating.

Learning to Speak

General

8. Aitchison, Jean, *The Articulate Mammal*, Hutchinson, 1976. Excellent introduction to Psycholinguistics.
9. Britton, James, *Language and Learning*, Penguin, 1970. Well-written, illuminating essay.
10. Stork, E. C. and Widdowson, J. D. A., see Chapter 1, 14 above.

Specialist

11. Bruner, J. S. and Connolly, K. J., *The Development of Competence in Early Childhood*, Academic Press, 1974. Authoritative.
12. Davies, A. (ed.), *Language and Learning in Early Childhood*, Heinemann, 1977. Excellent technical studies.
13. Derrick, June, *The Child's Acquisition of Language*, National Foundation for Educational Research, 1976. Useful.
14. Rogers, Sinclair (ed.), *Children and Language*, OUP, 1975. Useful readings.
15. Weir, Ruth, *Language in the Crib*, Mouton, 1962. Excellent, original work.

Educational Disadvantage

General

16. Bernstein, Basil, (gen. ed.), *Primary Socialization, Language and Education*, Routledge and Kegan Paul. An important series of monographs.
17. Cashdan, A., (ed.) *Language, Reading and Learning*, Blackwell, 1979. Essays on various aspects of language and learning.
18. Creber, J. W. P., *Lost for Words*, Penguin, 1972. Useful introduction.
19. *Language of Failure, The*, in *English in Education*, Vol. 4, No. 3, 1970. Some excellent papers.
20. Lawton, Denis, *Social Class, Language and Education*, Routledge and Kegan Paul, 1968. Excellent clear exposition.
21. Trudgill, Peter, see Chapter 1, 22 above.

Pedagogical

22. Cooper, Jean, Moodley, Molly, and Reynell, Joan, *Helping Language Development*, Edward Arnold, 1978. A remedial programme.
23. Gahagan, D. M. and G. A., *Talk Reform*, Routledge and Kegan Paul, 1970. A specific approach, worth reading about.
24. *Handbook: 0–5 years*, National Children's Bureau, 1977. A guide to stages of development.
25. *Handicapped Child and his Mother in the Playgroup, The*, Pre-school Playgroups Association, 1974. Useful guidance.
26. *Handicapped Children in Playgroups*, Pre-school Playgroups Association, 1976. Practical Guidance.
27. Hewett, Sheila, *The Family and the Handicapped Child*, Allen and Unwin, 1970. On cerebral palsied children.
28. *Language Development and the Disadvantaged Child*, Holmes McDougall for the Schools Council. Activities and guidance for teaching.
29. Mortenstern, M. *et al., Practical Training for the Severely Handicapped Child*, Spastics Society/Heinemann, 1966. Advice and examples.

Specialist

30. Brennan, Mary, *Can Deaf Children Acquire Language?*, British Deaf News Supplement, 1976. Excellent technical essay.

Language and Thinking

General

31. Boyle, D. G., see Chapter 2, 1 above. Concise chapter on Behaviorism, Piaget, etc.
32. Bruner, J. S., *Toward a Theory of Instruction*, Harvard University Press, 1966. Bruner's theory introduced by himself.
33. Donaldson, Margaret, *Children's Minds*, Fontana, 1978. A brilliant critical discussion.
34. Pulaski, Mary Ann, *Understanding Piaget*, Harper and Row, 1971. Introduces the main principles of Piaget's theories.

Specialist

35. Davies, A. (ed.), see Chapter 2, 12 above. Valuable essays by Roger Wales, Joan Tough and others.
36. Davies, A. (ed.), *Problems of Language and Learning*, Heinemann, 1975. Collection of papers on various topics, including Bruner's 'Language as an Instrument of Thought and Halliday's 'Talking One's Way In'.
37. Francis, Hazel, *Language in Teaching and Learning*, Allen and Unwin, 1977. Excellent study of language learning.
38. Keene, G. B., *Language and Reasoning*, Nostrand, 1963. A simple non-technical introduction, somewhat dated.
39. Piaget, Jean, *Language and Thought of the Child*, Routledge and Kegan Paul, 1960. First published 1926, still very readable though difficult.
40. Tough, Joan, *Focus on Meaning*, Allen and Unwin, 1973. Excellent introduction with practical guidance for teachers.
41. Vygotsky, L. S., *Thought and Language*, M.I.T. Press, 1962. Valuable exposition of Vygotsky's theories, but somewhat difficult.

Pedagogical

42. *New Era, The*, Vol. 59, No. 3, May/June 1978. Contains articles on Piaget and an annotated bibliography.
43. Solomon, Julia, *Learning to Think*, Kindergarten Association of Western Australia, 1973. Analysis of cognitive growth for nursery school teachers.
44. Solomon, Julia, *Encounters*, Child Study Publication, Western Australia, 1976. A schedule for nursery school teachers.
45. Tough, Joan, *Listening to Children Talking*, Ward Lock, 1976. Advice on appraising language skills and needs.
46. Tough, Joan, *Talking and Learning*, Ward Lock, 1977. On promoting communication skills in nursery and infants classrooms.

3. The Development of Language Skills

General

1. Jones, A., and Mulford, J. (ed.), *Children Using Language*, OUP, 1971. Excellent introductory papers.
2. *A Language for Life*, (The Bullock Report), HMSO, 1975. A major report.

Speech, Talk and Listening

Theoretical

3. Coulthard, Malcolm, *An Introduction to Discourse Analysis*, Longman, 1977. Authoritative account of speech acts, etc.
4. Wilkinson, A. *et al.*, *The Quality of Listening*, Macmillan, 1974. Discussion of research and development.

Pedagogical

5. Britton, James (ed.), *Talking and Writing*, Methuen, 1967. Papers on language learning, talk, etc.
6. *Children Talking*, in *English in Education*, Vol. 12, No. 2, 1978. Published by National Association for the Teaching of English.
7. Meers, Hilda J., *Helping Our Children Talk,* Longman, 1976. One of a series on early childhood education.
8. Rosen, Connie and Harold, *The Language of Primary School Children*, Penguin, 1973. Material on language learning.
9. Tough, Joan. See Chapter 2, 45 and 46 above.
10. Wilkinson, Andrew, *Spoken English*, University of Birmingham, 1965. Papers on speech and listening.

Reading

Theoretical

11. Diehl, William, *et al.,* (eds.), *Secondary Reading: Theory and Application*, Indiana University, 1978. Papers on various aspects of reading in the secondary school.
12. Levin, H., and Williams, Joanna P., (eds.), *Basic Studies in Reading*, Basic Books, New York, 1970. Important papers on research and theory.
13. Morris, Ronald, *Success and Failure in Learning to Read*, Penguin, 1973. Expanded edition of Morris's 1963 survey of reading methods.
14. Mour, Stanley I. (ed.), *Theoretical and Practical Consideration in Development of Reading Comprehension*, in *Viewpoints in Teaching and Learning*, Vol. 54, No. 3, 1978, Indiana University. Conference papers of varied importance, some of high value.
15. Pugh, A. K., *Silent Reading*, Heinemann, 1978. Excellent study of reading strategies.
16. Rankin, Earl F., *The Measurement of Reading Flexibility*, International Reading Association, 1974. Excellent objective study of research techniques in reading strategies, etc.
17. Smith, Frank, *Understanding Reading,* Holt, Rinehart and Winston, 1971. Brilliant psycholinguistic analysis of reading processes.
18. Smith, F. (ed.), *Psycholinguistics and Reading,* Holt, Rinehart and Winston, 1973. Research papers and the psycholinguistic approach.
19. Stauffer, R. G., *Learning to Read as a Thinking Process*, Harper Row, 1969. Stimulating theoretical discussion.
20. Vernon, M. D., *Reading and Its Difficulties*, CUP, 1971. A psychological study, thorough and useful.

Pedagogical

21. Cashdan, A. (ed.), See Chapter 2, 17 above.
22. Clark, M., and Milne, A. (eds.), *Reading and Related Skills,* Ward Lock, 1973. Some interesting discussions of reading teaching.

23. Dean, Joan, *Reading, Writing and Talking*, A. & C. Black, 1968. Excellent general advice on all three aspects.
24. International Reading Association publications. IRA, 800 Barksdale Road, Newark, Delaware 19711. All American teachers should subscribe.
25. Mackay, D., Thompson, Brian, and Schaub, Pamela, *Breakthrough to Literacy Teacher's Manual*, Longman, 1970. Introduction to the 'sentence methods' of teaching reading.
26. Moyle, D., *The Teaching of Reading*, Ward Lock, 1976. Excellent introductory survey.
27. Moyle, Donald, compiled by, *Teaching Reading*, Holmes McDougall, 1978. A seminar kit for in-service training.
28. *Reading* – official organ of the United Kingdom Reading Association. Published three times a year to members. All teachers should subscribe.
29. Robertson, H. Alan (ed.), *Reading and the Language Arts,* University of Chicago Press, 1963. Volume 25 of a long and valuable series of conference transactions.
30. Southgate, Vera, *Beginning Reading*, University of London Press, 1972. Excellent short survey of current methods and textbooks.

Writing

General

31. Britton, James and others, *The Development of Writing Abilities,* 11–18, Macmillan, 1975. A key study of the writing and teaching process.
32. Dixon, John, *Growth through English*, OUP, 1967. Thoughtful discussion of aims and techniques.
33. Gelb, I. J., *A Study of Writing*, University of Chicago Press, 1963. A classic study of the use and evolution of writing.
34. *Language for Life, A.* See Chapter 3, 2 above. Chapter 2 contains some useful notes on writing.

Pedagogical

35. Brown, T. M., and Millar, Robert, *Put it in Writing*, Heinemann, 1969. Useful guidance for students.
36. Burgess, Carol, *et al, Understanding Children Writing*, Penguin, 1973. Useful guidance and illustrative material.
37. Doughty, P., Pearce, J. and Thornton, G., *Language in Use*, Edward Arnold, 1971. A programme of language study and writing tasks.
38. Hyde, S. and Brown, W. H., *Composition of the Essay,* Addison-Wesley, 1967. For maturer students, a course in composition and style.
39. Marland, M., *et al., Language Across the Curriculum*, Heinemann, 1977. Some excellent guidance for teachers.
40. Martin, Nancy, *et al., Writing and Learning Across the Curriculum*, Ward Lock, 1976. Excellent guidance for teachers.

Spelling

Theoretical

41. Scragg, D. G., *A History of English Spelling*, Manchester University Press, 1974, and Harper and Row, 1974. Authoritative account of its development.
42. Venezky, Richard L., *The Structure of English Orthography*, Mouton, 1970. Brilliant authoritative study.

Pedagogical

43. *Language for Life, A.* See Chapter 3, 2 above. Chapter 2, Annex A, is a useful discussion of spelling in the classroom.
44. Peters, Margaret L., *Spelling: Caught or Taught?*, Routledge and Kegan Paul, 1967. Widely used, stimulating and practical.
45. Peters, Margaret L., *Diagnostic and Remedial Spelling Manual*, Macmillan, 1975. Useful practical guidance.

Punctuation

46. Carey, G. V., *Mind the Stop*, 1939. Somewhat dated but still useful.
47. Treble, H. A., and Vallins, *ABC of English Usage,* OUP, 1937. Still a most useful guide to punctuation, diction and usage.
48. Vallins, G. H., *Good English*, Pan 1951. Contains a useful chapter on punctuation.

4. Grammar, Rhetoric and Diction

Grammar

Theoretical

1. Chomsky, Noam, *Syntactic Structures*, Mouton, 1957.
2. Chomsky, Noam, *Current Issues in Linguistic Theory*, Mouton, 1964. Difficult and technical but still the most authoritative exposition of Chomskyan grammar.
3. Hasan, Ruqaiya, *Grammatical Cohesion in Spoken and Written English*, Longman, 1968. Part of the Schools Council Programme in Linguistics and English Teaching: highly technical but illuminating.

Pedagogical

4. Allen, J. P. B. and Corder, S. Pit. (eds.), *Papers in Applied Linguistics*, OUP, 1976. The chapter 'Grammar and Language Teaching' is valuable.
5. Brown, M. L., White, E. G. and Jenkinson, E. B., *Two Approaches to Teaching Syntax*, Indiana University Press, 1967. From the Indiana University English Curriculum Study Center: a most useful teaching guide.

6. Currie, William B., *New Directions in Teaching English Language*, Longman, 1973. Interesting account of the development of school grammar and of modern approaches.
7. Gleason, H. A., Jr., *Linguistics and English Grammar,* Holt, Rinehart and Winston, 1965. Easily the best and most thorough book on school grammars.
8. Mittins, W. H., *A Grammar of Modern English*, Methuen, 1962. Dated, but still worth using for its insights to sentence structure.
9. Roberts, Paul, *English Sentences*, Harcourt Brace, 1962. Excellent practical analyses of sentences.
10. Thomas, Owen, *Transformational Grammar and the Teacher of English*, Holt, Rinehart and Winston, 1965. Excellent school grammar based on TG, but difficult.

Rhetoric

11. Currie, William B. See Chapter 4, 6 above.
12. Graves, Robert and Hodge, Alan, *The Reader Over Your Shoulder*, Jonathan Cape, 1943. Excellent, entertaining guide to good English composition.
13. Millar, Robert and Currie, Ian, *The Language of Prose*, Heinemann, 1972. Excellent study of good prose and writing techniques.
14. Quirk, Randolph. See Chapter 1, 11 above. Some interesting chapters and exercises.

Diction

15. Copley, J., *Shift of Meaning*, OUP, 1961. Interesting discussion of 250 words whose meanings have changed.
16. Gowers, Sir Ernest, *Plain Words*, HMSO, 1954. Old-fashioned but entertaining and comprehensive essay on 'good English'.
17. Vallins, G. H. See Chapter 3, 48 above. Good chapter on cliché.

5. The Englishes of the World

General
1. Baugh, Albert, and Cable, Thomas. See Chapter 1, 24 above.

Dialects

2. Gregory, Michael and Carroll, Susanne, *Language and Situation*, Routledge and Kegan Paul, 1978. Valuable short introduction but difficult.
3. Labov, William, *The Study of Non-Standard English*, NCTE, 1970. Excellent discussion of social dialects.
4. Lado, Robert, *Linguistics Across Cultures,* University of Michigan Press

1957. Valuable technical guidance for teachers.
5. Macaulay, R. K. S., *Language, Social Class and Education*, Edinburgh University Press, 1977. An authoritative account of social dialects and their relationship with schooling.
6. McDavid, Raven I., Jr., *American Social Dialects*, NCTE, 1965. Two articles written for teachers.
7. McIntosh, Angus, *Introduction to a Survey of Scottish Dialects*, Nelson, 1961. An excellent brief introduction to dialectology.
8. Pride, J. B. and Holmes, Janet (eds.), See Chapter 1, 19 above.
9. Trudgill, Peter. See Chapter 1, 22 above.

American English

10. Strevens, Peter, *British and American English*, Cassell, 1978. A most useful short account of differences.

Australian and New Zealand English

11. Ramson, W. S. (ed.), *English Transported*, Australian National University Press, 1970. The best readily available collection of papers.

Other Englishes

12. Bailey, R. W. and Robinson, J. L., *Varieties of Present-Day English*, Macmillan, 1973. Collection of authoritative excerpts and studies.

6. The Uses of English

English and Situation

1. Enkvist, N. E., Spencer, J. and Gregory, M. J., *Linguistics and Style*, OUP, 1964. Useful introductory essays.
2. Gregory, Michael and Carroll, Susanne. See Chapter 5, 2 above.
3. Leech, Geoffrey N., *A Linguistic Guide to English Poetry*, Longman, 1969. Brilliant and original study of the subject.
4. Leech, Geoffrey N., *English in Advertising*, Longman, 1966. An excellent and informative account of advertising English.
5. Nash, Walter, *Our Experience of Language*, Batsford, 1971. A discussion of language and social behaviour.

Correctness

6. Philp, Andrew M., *Attitudes to Correctness in English*, Longman, 1968. Useful account of various notions and attitudes.
7. Wilkinson, Andrew (ed.), *The State of Language*, University of Birmingham, 1969. Vol. 22, No. 1 of *Educational Review*; contains 'What is Correctness' by W. H. Mittins.

Index